ALL QUESTIONS
GREAT AND SMALL

All Questions Great and Small

A *Seriously Funny* Book

ADRIAN PLASS AND JEFF LUCAS

HODDER &
STOUGHTON

First published in Great Britain in 2015 by Hodder & Stoughton
An Hachette UK company

1

A CIP catalogue record for this title is available from the British Library

ISBN 978 1 444 79316 1
eBook ISBN 978 1 444 79317 8

Typeset in Sabon by Hewer Text UK Ltd, Edinburgh

Printed and bound in the UK by CPI Group (UK) Ltd, Croydon CR0 4YY

Hodder & Stoughton policy is to use papers that are natural, renewable
and recyclable products and made from wood grown in sustainable
forests. The logging and manufacturing processes are expected to
conform to the environmental regulations of the country of origin.

Hodder & Stoughton Ltd
Carmelite House
50 Victoria Embankment
London
EC4Y 0DZ

www.hodderfaith.com

To Nicki Rogers and Philippa Hanna, who have added
music, laughter and the best of company to our tours

CONTENTS

FOREWORD

NICKI

Over the past 15 years I've had the privilege of singing along-side some wonderful writers and speakers in many different formats and events. I love my job with a passion and know how fortunate I am. However, I have to be honest, not every event is a gripping experience. There have been occasions where I've finished singing, and quickly found a hideaway to read a book, or send an email or two until it's time for my next set. Terrible, I know. Shame on me.

However, four years ago, I was invited to be part of a tour called 'Seriously Funny' with two people who had really truly impacted me when I'd met them separately, so I was immediately hopeful that I would have less need to find hideaways for a week or two on tour with them.

Jeff Lucas and Adrian Plass between them have enough hilarity to make even the most dour person crack a smile, enough reality of life to talk honestly without trying to gloss over very difficult and painful subjects, and most importantly enough love to leave the hardest-hearted person feeling a little warmer inside.

The Seriously Funny tour did exactly what it said on the tin: it combined the serious and funny in a conversation between friends about the trials and reality of everyday life as a believer. And best of all, the audience got to be part of the dialogue.

The first half of every evening began with what felt like a fireside chat between friends. We all listened in to an unscripted conversation between Jeff and Adrian which covered subjects as varied as loss, doubt, faith, depression, dead hamsters, incontinence and anything else which randomly found its way into their heads and thus onto the stage that night.

During the second half I ventured away from my piano stool and read aloud the audience's confidential questions for Jeff and Adrian to answer – or at least pass comment on.

People poured their hearts out on paper with crushing honesty, and it is fair to say that we experienced a glimpse into what sometimes felt like a battlefield of bruised, battered and occasionally really seriously wounded members of the beautiful and messy family of God.

Jeff and Adrian responded with honesty and grace, from their own experience, and at times, as they freely admitted, had no answers at all. No question was barred, and I worked hard to fire as many tricky ones their way as possible!

Of course, there was hilarity as well and quite often I watched people laugh through their tears, proving that laughter is indeed a good medicine. Tense shoulders started to relax all around the room as people realized they were exactly the same as the next person, and that the people on the stage were human too. At the end of each night there was a sense that a room full of strangers went home feeling a little more like perhaps they could belong. Perhaps they weren't so alone after all.

This book is a collection of those questions and a chance to capture again the feel of those serious and yet funny evenings.

I loved having the privilege of sharing a stage with two of my absolute favourite people in the world. What you see is what you get, and what you get is gold. Needless to say, no emails were sent during my evenings with Jeff and Adrian and I never once hid myself away on tour.

I'd suggest you turn your phone off, settle down in a cosy corner, and let your shoulders relax as you join in for this next step on the Seriously Funny journey.

Nicki Rogers

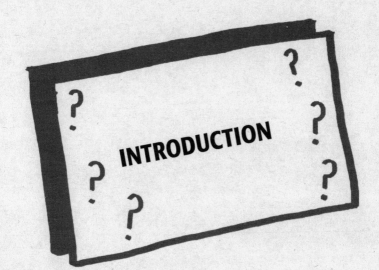

INTRODUCTION

Have you noticed the current fashion in Christian circles for emphatic, almost rollicking agreement with negatives? Want some examples? Okay.

'What do you think about doubt? Is it all right for Christians to doubt?'

'Oh, yes! Yes! Yes! Oh, my goodness, yes! Doubt is essential. If you don't doubt, faith is meaningless! Never give up your doubt. It is when we doubt that true belief is most in evidence.'

'Why does God seem to ignore my prayers?'

'Because he cares for you, of course. How else are you to learn trust? These are God-given opportunities to believe you are loved without being given what you want. Grasp those opportunities and be thankful.'

'I find church a bit boring.'

'A bit boring? Church is the most tedious, jaw-droppingly awful way to spend time that any sane person could possibly imagine. The buildings, the music, the services, the people, the ministers, the prayer, the worship, the coffee, the quiche, all mindlessly uninteresting and yawn-making. Bask in the sunlight of your divinely inspired insight. Now you can begin to move forward! Congratulations!'

'God hates sin, doesn't he?'

'Hates sin? God? Good gracious, you're not really getting yourself caught up in that nonsense, are you? Sin is the shadow thrown by the light of God's purity. Something to be valued and learned from. Let's get real. God uses sin.'

A bit of an exaggeration, but the fashion or phase is a real one. Why? What is going on? My suggestion is that more and more people are becoming aware of the conceptual and creative shallowness that tends to characterise the things we say and write about Christian experience. Diving down into the shadowy depths of denial may be an attempt to stir up mud in the hope that something new and with its own gritty substance could float to the surface.

Perhaps we have been a little lazy about giving proper attention to the questions that are so often asked by those who are seeking a truth that genuinely meshes with reality. Jeff and I have expressed this view more than once in the past. Over the last few years we have toured together on a number of occasions, publicising new books and engaging in unplanned dialogue for the first half of each evening. The second half offered an opportunity for the audience to ask us any question at all, and certainly challenged us to put our money where our big (some might say overactive) mouths are. Folk were not backward at coming forward, as my mother used to say. Our task was to respond to these funny, heartfelt, inquisitive, desperate queries as honestly and as helpfully as possible. Most of this book is based on those questions, and our struggling attempts to remain authentic and vaguely entertaining in our replies.

Negative? Positive? Hard-to-digest but ultimately valuable? Helpful? Probably all of those things in varying measure, but you must judge for yourselves. Christianity has never been an exact science, but we do hope you appreciate our very personal outpourings.

Adrian Plass

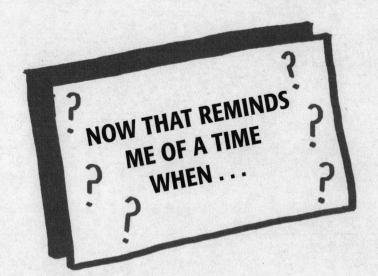

NOW THAT REMINDS
ME OF A TIME
WHEN . . .

Will pets go to heaven?

Before we get started on this, let me just say that I am fully aware of the hamster issue. As my wife rightly points out, hamsters have some kind of design fault (sorry, God, but they do). They die. They disappear. They go off on excursions to the underneath and back and inside of places that are dangerous for them. Bad things happen to these fluffy little creatures. A friend of mine told me that her young granddaughter texted her one day to announce that she had two new hamsters, and had christened them 'Faith' and 'Hope'. All very sweet and biblical, of course, but perhaps they needed a 'Charity' to complete the set. A subsequent text conveyed the unexpected and rather bizarre news that Faith had eaten Hope.

'Hope has died, but faith remains' might be an encouraging message in other contexts, but not in this Tarantino-style episode in a small child's life.

The point I'm making is that, in terms of human understanding, if pets are to be saved, heaven must presumably offer a veritable sea, an endless vista, an eternity of small

3

brown squeaking things waiting to be reclaimed by their resurrected owners. This is, of course, quite apart from the legions of rabbits, dogs, cats, horses, donkeys, elephants, camels and other assorted creatures that have been cherished by human beings at some stage in their lives. It all begins to seem rather wearyingly absurd, doesn't it?

However, if we are prepared, by an act of the will, to abandon temporarily the tedious limits of human understanding, there may be another path to explore. Access to this path has only opened up for me since I began to catch a glimpse of the way in which love, whimsy and ingenuity operate together in the nature of God. I find this hard enough to comprehend myself, let alone pass on to anyone else, but I will have a go.

A glance at the ministry of St Paul helps. Clearly, the great apostle felt quite free to change the shape and approach of his ministry whenever such change was helpful to the task in hand. The altar dedicated TO AN UNKNOWN GOD in Athens is a good example. Thank goodness there wasn't a local committee of earnest evangelicals with a veto over Paul's decision to identify this deity without a name as the one true God and Father of the resurrected Jesus. Great idea, wasn't it? The sort of bespoke great idea that I believe God still wants to use in his dealings with men and women in this age. Unexpected, slightly cranky, faintly disturbing, non-religious, individual, cherishing, charmingly whimsical and inventive, these ideas do not necessarily fit into the man-made shapes that are so common to our all-too-impoverished ministry. I know a man who never really enjoyed using his workshop because he got so neurotic whenever one of the carefully drawn shapes on his wall was missing its

4

appropriate hammer or chisel or screwdriver. I think he might have preferred to simply sit happily in the middle of his carefully ordered workshop and never actually use the tools at all. Much safer. Remind you of anything? Yes? I thought it might.

So, what does all this have to do with pets? Well, one very parochial event in 2012 dominates my memory of that year. It was a death, the death of a dog belonging to friends of ours: A massive, velvety-grey Great Dane, Buddy had a huge personality, an incredible appetite and an unquenchable instinct for loving and for being loved.

Dave and Faith and Ruth and Jonny were devastated by their loss, and it was truly difficult for all of us to believe that such a massive presence could simply cease to exist.

After Buddy's death someone asked me if I thought there would be dogs in heaven. What would you have said? In this postmodern age we all seem to pluck beliefs and convictions out of the air and give them credence simply because they find a home in us. I have no idea if animals will be in heaven, but I do know two things for sure. Love cannot be destroyed. That's one. The other is that, as I've already said, God is full of wise, whimsical ideas and will do exactly what he wants. Bearing those things in mind, I decided to write a poem, and this was it.

Buddy

His head was as big as a shoebox,
Eyes like a curious child,
Feet spread like mops, slobbering chops,
Deaf to the call of the wild.

There happened to be a big meeting,
In heaven the day Buddy died,
From early to late, the ancient debate,
Should pets be permitted inside?

Most angels said, 'No, they don't have a soul,
The concept is wrong and absurd.'
A dozen or more were not quite so sure,
But God sat, and spoke not a word.

At last he arose, and said, 'I propose,
Next month we continue to talk,
But dusk is fast falling, the hillside is calling,
And Buddy is needing a walk.'

Jeff, you live in the USA, where there are a lot of guns. Have you ever found yourself staring down the barrel of one?

Yes. Twice.

The first time I got acquainted with the business end of a gun was in Reno, Nevada. I was driving on what I thought was the inside lane of the freeway, which it was not. Apparently I was driving on the hard shoulder, and so a local cop decided that he and I should have a little chat. He came speeding up behind me, with his lights flashing red and blue. In those days at least, back in England, if a member of the local constabulary wanted to pull you over, they would overtake you, and then switch on an illuminated sign that said 'Stop'. In America they don't use that sign, but just flash those lights from behind you. US-based cop shows were not that widespread back then, so I was unaware that this law enforcement person wanted to talk to me. I thought he wanted to get by. So I slowed down, but carried on driving.

Then he put his siren on. I still didn't understand. I kept driving.

Then came a searchlight, mounted on the roof, shining in my mirror. Yet I drove on.

Now irate, the cop finally got my attention by yelling through the PA system from his car, 'Stop the car, right now!' At that point I felt led to stop the car, right then. But my troubles were just beginning.

In the UK, it's the done thing to get out of the car to speak to the officer – at least it used to be. Happily, I've not had too many roadside chats with the splendid women and men who serve in our police force recently, so I don't know if this is still the case. But in America you *don't* get out of the car, because that's viewed as a threat. Here's my advice, if this ever happens to you in the US of A. Lower your window. Wait calmly for the officer. Place your hands on the steering wheel, where he or she can see them. And when asked for your driving licence, don't make a sudden lunge for the glove-box, because it might look like you're reaching for a gun, which could lead to some unpleasant consequences. I was unaware of all this roadside etiquette, and leapt out of the car.

That's when I heard the cop yell, 'Freeze! Stay right there!' He had that spotlight on me, and I could see him silhouetted in the glaring light, feet planted, arms extended, gun in hand, pointed at my head. Not nice.

I decided to become the blustering Englishman, and did my very best impersonation of Prince Charles. It worked a treat.

The other, more chilling occasion was when our family got shot at. It was a friend who did it, and a pastor at that. Very impolite.

Also a Brit living in America, John had bought himself a .308 rifle, which is a very serious weapon indeed. Kay and I, together with our young family at the time, were over at John's house for breakfast. Suddenly he leapt up from the table, gleefully insisting that he had something he wanted us to see.

Returning momentarily from his bedroom, he brandished his new acquisition, the rifle. He was determined to show us how it worked, and besides, he said, it wasn't loaded, obviously.

He was wrong. I don't know why, but for some reason he had put some bullets in the magazine and then forgotten that he had done so. Cocking the rifle, he pulled the trigger. The sound of the bullet being discharged in the confined space of that kitchen was deafening. The bullet hit the wood stove at the end of the dining table, and then ricocheted across the middle of the table, ending up in the ceiling. It missed us by a metre at the most.

We looked around the table, tearfully wondering if our children were still alive.

They were traumatised, but safe.

John ran into the bedroom, in shock himself, and in a frantic attempt to make the rifle safe, he put another bullet into the chamber and shot a hole in the carpet. At this point his wife ran into the bedroom, yelling that he needed to get out of the house and not come back until that gun was empty of bullets.

When the police officer wants you to stop, pull over.

And when a Brit with a gun wants you to stop by for breakfast, don't go round, whatever you do.

What's the worst meal that you've had to pretend you liked?

Eating Ethiopian food in Ethiopia (where I suppose it's just called food). I'm not indicting their national cuisine, it was probably just the restaurant we ate at, but there were three reasons for choosing this as my all-time least-favourite meal.

Ethiopian culture calls for honoured guests to be fed by their host, so the chap next to me starting picking up my food (with his fingers, no utensils in sight) and shoving it into my mouth. I was too polite to decline, although the temptation to bite his fingers was intense (a bit too Hannibal Lecter). And I was panicking, too, because in that culture one hand is used for scooping up food, and the other is used for wiping one's . . . no, I said I'd never mention that subject again. Let's just say, I was terrified he was using the wrong hand.

And then one of our group was terribly sick after he had wolfed down copious amounts of said food. It wasn't pretty.

Finally, we had something called *injera* to eat, which looks like human skin. It may even taste like human skin, for all I know. Must ask Hannibal Lecter.

Yuck.

Do you have any funny stories about health and safety?

Yes, I do have an incredibly funny story about health and safety. Unfortunately, this wonderful tale is so rib-shatteringly, thigh-slappingly hilarious that I have been banned from writing, speaking or in any other way sharing it with any other human being, by DISMAL, the Department for Immediate Suppression of Manic, Asinine Laughter. The penalty for contravention is death, and I'm not going to risk that again. I had an excruciating experience with them when I failed to entertain a hall filled with people at a Round Table meeting in Ashby-de-la-Zouch in 1997. Never again.

Jeff may have a less funny story that he is allowed to tell you. I believe DISMAL have given him a season pass.

Jeff, as a seasoned traveller, do you have any advice for long-haul flights?

First of all, be grateful that you have the opportunity to experience travel. I mean it. In India, there's a retired aircraft engineer who has a redundant plane in his backyard. Every day he allows people from his village to come and experience a virtual flight. They board, strap themselves in, go through a safety briefing, and then, after being served snacks, they disembark – having gone nowhere. Their poverty means that none of these people are ever likely to fly anywhere. When I'm tempted to huff and puff about delays, mechanical breakdowns, moody flight attendants who seem like they're itching to zap their passengers with cattle prods, or in-flight food that is unrecognisable and only vaguely edible, or when the chap in front of me cuts off my circulation by putting his seat back, I try to remember that village in India.

And then, when things go wrong, be nice. That's not only a thoroughly Christian idea, it works well from an altruistic point of view as well. I've seen people cursing and yelling at check-in desks, demanding different seats, huffing and puffing over delays or cancellations, and expecting the person they're bullying to go out of their way to help them, which they almost certainly will not.

Once I had an amazing experience on a British Airways flight. I had a very cheap economy class ticket from Denver to London, and on check-in I was told that I was being upgraded to business class and could therefore use the airline lounge before boarding. I was thrilled to bits, and almost skipped into the lounge. The receptionist noticed my chirpy demeanour and asked me why I was so happy.

'I'm delighted because I've been upgraded today. It's brilliant!'

'That's nice,' she grinned, and then surprised me with her next comment.

'Often people who get upgraded start becoming aggressive and demanding when they get to the lounge. Even though their upgrade was free, they feel entitled, more important, and haughty. It's nice to see someone who is grateful.'

I sat down, grabbed a coffee. Twenty minutes later, the receptionist headed over towards me. 'Give me your boarding pass, please, Mr Lucas. I need to move you.'

My face fell, my heart sank. 'Oh no! Am I being downgraded now?' I ventured.

'No. You're being upgraded again. First class. I just got a call from the plane, and they need to move somebody into the front. As you were so grateful, and nice to me, I thought of you. Enjoy it.'

And enjoy it I did. I almost wept when the flight landed, the experience had been so amazing.

Jeff, have you got an embarrassing funeral anecdote?

Not exactly. I do know of someone who must have been terribly embarrassed about one funeral that I led. And that's because he was supposed to lead it himself, but he totally forgot all about it. I won't say which denomination he came from (that would be unfair to Salvation Army officers the world over), but suffice to say I got a phone call from the local crematorium, with a funeral director on the other end of the line who sounded very panicked indeed.

'What are you doing right now, Jeff?'

At that moment I had been doing some gardening, which is weird, because that's probably the only hour of my life that I've ever spent working in the garden. (Except to cut the grass. That doesn't count.) When I touch living things, they wither and die.

'Do you think you could throw your suit on and get over here? I have mourners, impatient undertakers, and a coffin with a body in it, but no one to officiate. The minister who was booked has obviously forgotten, and I can't get hold of him. You need to come quickly.'

And so I did. It was awkward, to say the least, because I had to walk quietly up to the primary mourners who were sitting on the front row of the packed funeral chapel, to ask the name of the deceased and a few details about his life before performing the obligatory despatch. They were obviously upset and angry, but grateful for my help.

I was glad to do it.

And I was also very glad that I was not the chap who had forgotten that most important appointment. I can only hope *he* lived to see another day.

Adrian, if we had a function at our church, would you do it for seventy pounds?

I might. I might do it for nothing. I might ask for quite a lot more. In the thirty years since I was first (to my amazement) paid real money for standing up and talking to people, I have never found it easy to talk about fees and things. I suspect that I might have got a bit ripped off once or twice in the early days, largely because I found it hard to believe that I actually had a product to offer.

I do recall shooting myself in the foot a couple of times.

In the very early 1990s, for instance, someone rang me up one morning to ask if I was willing and available to speak at a meeting arranged to celebrate the opening of a new church extension. A quick glance at our wall calendar showed that the date fitted well, but there was one more query to answer. The dialogue went something like this:

HIM: Just one more thing, Adrian. Can you give us some idea of how much you want to charge for the event?

ME: (squirming with embarrassment, and wondering if *I* ought to pay *them* for being kind enough to invite me) Er, let me see – seventy-five pounds would be fine, thanks.

HIM: (clearly very surprised) Seventy-five pounds!

ME: (miserably, since I had obviously asked for far too much) Oh, well, actually fifty pounds would be more than enough . . .

HIM: I'm just a bit taken aback. The last person I asked wanted fifteen hundred pounds. No, seventy-five is OK with me.

I bet it was – and who could blame him? But I was a bit fed up with myself. We weren't all that well off at the time, and my greedy little mind kept playing with the idea that if I had been mad enough to ask for the astronomical sum of one thousand pounds, the chap on the phone might have said, 'Gosh, yes, that sounds very reasonable. Thanks very much.'

As it happens, I know that he would not have reacted in that way, because I later learned that his first port of call had been Roy Castle, a big name in the world of secular entertainment, and much in demand at Christian events. Shortly before his untimely death, I encountered Roy during a charity event held at the Palladium. He was the lead act, and my role was very minor indeed, but it was good to meet such a fine ambassador for the faith, however briefly. In case you're wondering, I didn't feel it was necessary to mention my seventy-five pounds stand-in fee.

Sometimes people are amazingly generous. In those early days Bridget and I spoke at a church on the south coast where the vicar was nearing retirement and wanted to put on an event where his congregation and other local Christians could simply relax and enjoy themselves. His church building was not huge, but on that evening there were three hundred folk packed into pews and spare chairs, all looking forward to a lot of laughter and perhaps a few tears. It was one of those evenings that shine in my memory, filled with goodwill and the glorious gift of unexpected togetherness. Heaven would have to up its game to compete with that.

Afterwards we spent some time with the vicar and his wife. They were good folk, wise in their simplicity and, we guessed, immensely rich in heaven.

'We weren't sure what to do about money,' said the minister, 'but we charged everyone three pounds to make it affordable, and three hundred tickets were sold, so we thought we might as well give it all to you.'

Leaning across, he placed nine hundred pounds in notes into my hand. Bridget and I sat and stared wide-eyed at this crunchy wad of cash. We had never seen anything like it, never held so much money in our hands at one time. It was a benevolent shock, and it made us feel like bursting into tears. So clean and simple. I can't remember which particular financial crisis it averted, but there must have been one. There always was in those days.

What am I talking about? There always is.

Contrast that experience with one where, after the event – an outdoor procession followed by a talk – I was approached by a very, very large young man holding a very, very small notebook, and a tiny pen like the ones that none of us Christians steal from Argos these days.

'I have been told to ask for your expenses,' he announced in a gruff monotone.

'Oh, right,' I replied, 'so do you want me to include some sort of fee in that, or—'

'I have been told to ask for your expenses!'

'Yes, I just wondered—'

'Your expenses!'

I was a pushover. I muttered something unhappily, and watched as the substantial young man breathed heavily through his nose with annoyance, made a note in his Lilliputian notebook and departed our presence without further question or comment. We never did get a fee for that event. It's a good job I'm a Christian, because, even now, I'd quite like to find that young man and kick him very hard in the back of his right knee when he's least expecting it.

By the way, while we're on this subject, some have doubted the veracity of a story I have told many times about a treasurer who approached the speaker after a meeting and said, 'We would like to fellowship in the petrol.' The speaker apparently replied, 'We can frolic in the Germolene as long as I get my expenses.' This may possibly be apocryphal. Popped in by the Catholics, no doubt.

Honestly!

In fact I am amazed by the number of memories that pop up as soon as I spend time thinking about this. How about this one? A lady wrote me a charmingly enthusiastic letter (in the days when people did such outmoded,

17

folksy things) asking if Bridget and I would be interested in coming to speak at her place of worship, an Anglican church out in the middle of the countryside. Would we come, and how much would we charge, because she would have to gain the agreement of her Parochial Church Council for the project. A few days later she telephoned to say, in a very crestfallen voice, that the PCC had vetoed her plans because they were unwilling to underwrite a fee that was too high to be recouped by such an event.

She sounded so sad and disappointed. It was like a red thingy to a whatsit. 'Never mind them,' we said, 'we'll come for nothing.' (That's the polite version.) 'You set it up, and we'll be there.'

That church really was in the middle of nowhere. To be fair to the PCC, it must have seemed unlikely that many people would turn up to listen to these two obscure characters who were going to blether on for ninety minutes, with a break in the middle for refreshments. It must have been difficult enough getting a small group to church for an hour on Sunday morning, let alone two hours on a Thursday night, when they could have been at home, cosily watching *The Bill*.

That church was packed, stuffed, jammed to the limit. I have no idea where they all came from, but I don't think I have ever seen less space available for Bridget and me to stand side by side. Not that we minded. It was wonderful. We like to be as close as possible to the groups we address, and some lucky occupiers of the front row that night would have been able to see right up my nose – if they had been strange enough to want that experience, I mean.

And the cherry on the – what is it you have a cherry on? I think I mean the icing on the cake. Ah, I've googled it, and apparently it can be the cherry on the cake, or the cherry on the top. Anyway, the icing on the cake or the cherry on the cake or the cherry on top of the icing on the cake, was an unexpected freewill offering taken for us at the church that evening, which collected considerably more than the amount we had asked for originally.

Life can be tricky, as we all know, but every now and then we are gifted with a moment that is so very sweet. Can you begin to imagine what a satisfying outcome that was for the dear lady who had invited us in the first place?

Generally speaking, we have encountered heart-warming generosity over the last three decades, and we freely forgive those miserable gits who have not considered our tent-making worthy of reward.

Finally, I feel special mention should be made of the minister who presented a friend of mine with a promising white envelope after he had spoken at a church event. Later, in his car, my friend opened the envelope to find a single slip of paper inscribed with the following inspirational words: 'It is more blessed to give than to receive.'

When you speak internationally, are there times when your humour gets lost in translation?

Often it does, yes. Completely.

I've written about this in one of the *Seriously Funny* books, but it bears repeating in this context . . . I once had the privilege of spending four days sharing Bible teaching with a group of Sri Lankan Tamil refugees who formed the majority of a church in Paris. I've already written about this. These marvellous people had taken time off work – many of them were on low incomes so this was at huge personal cost to them – so they could listen to me blethering on about the Bible. Few spoke English, so I was working with a translator. Tamil, by the way, is one of those languages where the English word 'hello' seems to take about five minutes to translate.

Anyway, I tried to pepper the long days with some humorous stories, and I was delighted that they always seemed to see the funny side, because every time they laughed loudly and on cue. It turns out that they were really being cued. Literally.

About half way through the conference, and in the middle of one of the sessions, I turned to the translator mid-flow and remarked that I was delighted my humour was being understood so well. I was shattered by her reply: 'They don't get your humour at all, Jeff. What's happening is that when you tell one of your little stories, I just say to them, "Jeff was just being funny then. Please laugh now."'

And laugh they did: loudly, enthusiastically. To order. How beautifully kind they were. I stopped telling my little 'funny' stories.

And then there was the time I was speaking to a Salvation Army international youth congress, in Prague. The layout of the huge hall looked like the United Nations, dotted with little translation booths, and clusters of nationals seated around each.

I tried one of my stories.

The Brits laughed first, as obviously no translation was needed. Thirty seconds later came the French. And then the Dutch.

But my most recent humour gaff – just a few days ago, as I write – was when I was preaching in Malaysia. Asians have high respect for leaders in their culture generally, and the church where I was preaching were incredibly respectful towards their leadership. I should have noticed that before launching into my story about a pastor who fell into an adult baptismal tank fully clothed. When I've told that story anywhere else in the world, people have laughed. But this time, when I got to the hapless cleric's watery fall, the whole congregation gasped in horror. This was a terrible calamity, a pastor tripping into the pool. Was the poor pastor going to be OK? Was he seriously hurt? For a moment I thought they were going to start a prayer meeting for the unknown vicar who got so wet. Not only were they concerned for his welfare, but the idea of laughing at his misfortune was quite unthinkable. The story sank like a stone, just like the pastor.

They couldn't see anything remotely amusing about his trip and fall.

Come to think of it, perhaps my Malaysian friends were right. Maybe it just wasn't funny.

Have you ever been booked to speak at a series of church meetings, and got cancelled halfway through because they were so upset with what you'd said?

Yes. It was awful.

Before I tell you that particular story, I should say that there are a couple of churches that have made it very clear that I should never darken their doors again. Once I was preaching a series of services for a church in the USA, quite unaware that they were going through some significant conflict with their pastor. Emergency deacons' meetings were being held each evening during the four days that I was with them, and by all accounts they were bruising times for all. The pastor, though, decided not to mention any of this to me. Each night, I'd go along to the service to preach, and during the sermon, quite by chance, I would home in on one of the issues that had been discussed in the hot and heavy deacons' meetings the night before. This happened four times in a row. The deacons became convinced that the pastor was tipping me off about the contentious issues, and that he had brought me in to fight his corner and fire off shots for him. They were very angry with me, and made it plain that I would never be welcome in their church again. I can't blame them, because if I had been a stooge, that would have been terrible.

I tried to convince them that the points I'd made might be neither the results of tip-offs nor coincidence, but the activity of the Holy Spirit – that perhaps these things were being raised because God wanted them raised. It was to no avail. It's a shame when we say we believe in an intervening God, but then refuse to believe that he's been at work when he intervenes. I have never been invited back.

That pales in comparison with what happened in Palermo, Sicily. I was out there taking part in an anti-Mafia march. Two judges had been slaughtered, and the evangelicals in Sicily decided that they wanted to express their outrage at Mafia control in their country. I was privileged to briefly address the gathered crowd in Palermo town square, and then was due to speak at a Pentecostal church in the morning. To my horror, I found that the women were forced to sit separate from the men, and had to wear long veils that covered their hair and shoulders.

After the service, I joined the pastor and some of his staff at his house for lunch. The pastor was a dab hand at making the most beautiful homemade wine, and it's fair to say that a good amount of it was going down everyone's throats. Conversation was tricky, not only because it was being conducted through a translator, but because, as the wine flowed, the volume around the table increased. Then came the following awkward dialogue between their senior leader and myself.

PASTOR: So, Brother Jeff, tell me – what do you think of our practice of requiring our women to wear the veil to cover their heads?

ME: (*More focused on thinking about trying to eat the deep-fried sea snake that sat uninvitingly on my plate*) If it's all right with you, Pastor, I'd rather not get into that right now. (OK, perhaps I was a coward, but I told myself that I was attempting to be culturally sensitive – and I didn't want to get into a theological fight so early in my visit.)

PASTOR: I really would like to know of your views. Please tell me.

ME: (*Surprised, both by the taste of the deep-fried sea snake – even more unpleasant than I'd thought – and also at the tenacity of my interrogative host*) I'd really prefer not to comment.

PASTOR: (*Hitting the table so hard his assistants jumped*) TELL ME RIGHT NOW WHAT YOU THINK! WHAT DO YOU THINK OF THE VEIL?

ME: (*Looking anxiously at the knife that sat prone beside his plate, and hoping that it was going to stay that way*) Well, seeing as you asked, sir, I don't like it at all. I think it's sexist, oppressive and represents an interpretation of Scripture that is flawed . . . I don't mean to be culturally insensitive or disrespectful, but . . .

PASTOR: (*Exploding into loud and vehement words that were, thankfully, incomprehensible to me, being in Italian*) . . .

The interpreter looked sheepish at the pastoral explosion. I flushed crimson red. The room went deathly quiet.

I managed to finish my meal without any further

conversation, and at its conclusion quietly excused myself and went to my room to rest. Two hours later, I came back out to the kitchen, where I was to meet another pastor, who had come to pick me up. I was due to speak at his church that night. He was waiting for me.

NEW PASTOR: Hello, Jeff. You may go back to your room now. We won't be needing you to preach at our church tonight.

ME: (*Confused, and pondering the possibility that this whole thing might be a bad dream*) Really? Why not?

NEW PASTOR: We have heard of your views about the veil. You will not be needed.

And with that, he turned and left. I went back to my room, and was taken to the airport the next day. The ride there was conducted in tense silence.

I don't like sexism, veils or leaders who shout. And, if I'm being honest, I don't really like deep-fried sea snake either.

What is the most embarrassing thing that has ever happened to you?

I could fill an entire book trying to answer that question, because there have been so many embarrassing episodes.

Parking my car in a packed airport car park and then

forgetting where I left it. I got to peruse thousands of cars.

Having a chalet maid pop her head around the door at a Christian conference. She said a cheery good morning and stared straight into my eyes – a fixed stare that I was most grateful for, seeing as I was stark naked.

Making comments about an extremely boring man who always 'did the notices' at a church that I visited. Over dinner with some new friends, I declared that the man was as dull as dishwater. They wouldn't know him, would they, seeing as that church was hundreds of miles away, and these people were from a different denomination? The lady who was hosting the evening smiled sweetly and exhibited great self-control. The awesomely boring man was her father.

Setting off a car alarm at 3 a.m. in a residential area, and watching the lights of a dozen houses come on. Imagining all those nice people waking up swearing. Hiding from the policeman who was called out to investigate the noise, because for ten minutes I couldn't find a way to turn the thing off. That alarm was probably heard on Jupiter.

Riding in the back seat of a beautiful BMW so sophisticated that the car battery was installed under the rear passenger seat. Earlier that day a new battery had been fitted, one that turned out to be the wrong size, so the terminals were protruding too high. I sat in the back and as the seat sank a little under my weight it connected the underwired base of the seat to the battery terminals. I smelled what I thought was oil, but it turned out that there was a fire burning beneath my bottom. We pulled the gorgeous car over, jumped out, and watched it go up in flames. Not a great day. Even though it was not my fault, it was my rear end that did the damage.

But one of the most publicly excruciating events happened when I was speaking at a Christian school in America. Some of the students had been unhelpfully inoculated against faith, the result of their having copious amounts of biblical information shoved down their throats (you know it's bad when the Maths teacher instructs you to add five loaves to two fishes). Some of the students were sitting in the chapel wearing a practised look of boredom on their faces.

I decided to play the British card. That usually does the trick in America.

Not that day.

I thought it would be fun to start off by talking about how we Brits pronounce words differently from our American cousins.

I could have picked any number of examples, but for some reason I couldn't think of one, and so I asked my audience, who by now were practising the new sport of synchronised yawning, a very silly question.

'How do you say "Yo"?' I enquired hopefully.

Yo was a cool word back in the 1980s. I was British, hip and cool. They'd like this.

A surly looking, spotty youth on the back row, looking stunned at the stupidity of this gormless British visitor, repeated the word 'Yo' back to me.

'Yo,' he said. 'We say it the same way you do.'

He paused, triumphant, allowing the frozen silence to chill the air, and then said it again.

'Yo.'

Unsurprisingly, after such an epic warm-up routine, the rest of the talk didn't go too well, except I think that one guy sitting on the front row experienced a healing.

Of insomnia.

WHERE'S MY
SOAPBOX?!

Why do I get judged for having a non-Christian boyfriend when I love him and he is good to me?

The words often quoted in connection with questions like this are to be found in the sixth chapter of the second book of Corinthians. 'Do not be yoked together with unbelievers . . .'

A number of things strike me. First of all, anyone who really is judging someone else's behaviour or spiritual status had better be careful. If I claim to live by the Bible I am not allowed to cherry-pick the bits I like and reject the commands that get in my way. Not judging others is a much more unambiguous injunction than the one about who you get yoked with. I suppose it's all about where your heart is. If I genuinely care about a person and feel that they might have taken a wrong direction, I might need to quietly express my view, but if I'm just a boring old bossy-boots Christian who enjoys telling people off I'd better get back in my box and stay there.

Yes, some Christians take a very simplistic view of that

31

verse in Corinthians. Believers should never embark on close relationships or marriage with anyone who is not of the same faith. Simple. And, as is so often the case with views that are increasingly unpopular, there is some sense in this argument. Bridget and I have been closely acquainted with couples whose relationships have become seriously damaged or even been destroyed by the continual strain placed on them through holding such widely differing views of the world. Some of the young Christians we know have made a decision to avoid this kind of potential conflict by resolving to marry within the Church. Good for them. I sincerely wish them the very best (especially the girls, who must survey the stock of appropriate and available Christian men with increasing dismay as the years pass by).

If only it was always that simple. It's not, of course. Take Bridget and me, for instance. When we met at the Bristol Old Vic Theatre School back in the 1970s, I was a strange, rabid evangelical, and Bridget had lost her early interest in the faith after arriving at university four years earlier to find that a belief in God was difficult to argue for and very far from cool. My motivation for pursuing a relationship with Bridget was certainly not spiritually based, but God, being the opportunist that he clearly is, somehow used the situation to bring her to faith and to establish a relationship that is still going strong after forty-four years. Were we unevenly yoked? Well, the lines may not be clearly defined as some like to suggest, but certainly I would have called myself a Christian, and I am pretty sure she would not. Did it matter? Not as far as we can see. The yoke pinches a little occasionally, but it's as strong as it ever was.

As I write, two close friends of ours come to mind. They have been married for even longer than us, and I remember them saying that the announcement of their engagement was received with horror by just about everybody. This was not a case of an unbeliever being yoked with a believer. It was far more disastrous than that. This match was set to make Armageddon look like a game of pat-a-cake. A Brethren brother marrying a Methodist? Not only were they from *separate congregations*, but also from *different denominations of the Christian Church*!

I gather that the members of each of those congregations were pretty certain they were the only ones going to heaven, and absolutely certain that the others were bound for the other place, or perhaps for some alternative denominational paradise. I kid you not.

These were twentieth-century churches, for goodness' sake! How on earth have we managed, so continually and without coercion, to step into such steaming piles of nonsense? Forgive us, Lord, we are such idiots at times.

I have another memory, this one a secure mounting block from which to ride off on a veritable stallion from among my stable of hobby-horses (don't sniff – it's called a metaphor).

This event happened more than thirty years ago, and I wrote about it at the time – but I hope it bears repeating in this context. A friend of mine, who was not a Christian at the time, asked me if I would speak at his father's cremation service. I was very fond of Ian and more than happy to help if I could, so on the night before the service I travelled to Brighton to learn as much as possible from Ian and his mum about the person they had loved so much. I discovered four significant facts about Frank.

First, he had brought real love into his wife's life for the first time. She had had a very religious upbringing. Lots of ritual. Many, many meetings. A great deal of church attendance. In the midst of all these formalities there was little trace of softness and love. Somehow her faith had survived, but her heart was starved.

Then, as a young adult, she met Frank, and everything changed. He was the first person to offer her genuine affection and warmth. They fell in love and were married.

The second aspect of Frank that I noted that evening was his gift for relating easily to people. Both in the community and at his place of work he had been known as a man who was able to help with the settlement of arguments and disputes.

Thirdly, he was a skilled carpenter.

It was the fourth piece of information about Ian's dad that caused me disquiet. It appeared that Frank had certainly not been a Christian in his lifetime, and would probably have resented any attempt to, as his wife put it, 'stick that label on him after his death'. And who could blame him?

I didn't sleep very well that night. Morning was coming at me like a driverless express train and I was no nearer to finding an answer to my own question. What point could I make at the end of my address without compromising Frank's absence of faith, or my own sense that Jesus needed to be in on the act in some way? Lying awake that night, I was dismally aware of how impoverished Christian communication and language tends to be. I was still asking God for ideas as I fell asleep.

I sometimes think that the night shift in my brain works harder and better than the lazy old daytime crowd. When

I woke in the morning I knew exactly how to end my address. I made a note at the time that it seemed to be printed on some kind of mental ticker-tape. All I had to do was copy it down on the piece of paper beside my bed and then commit it to memory.

Later that morning the time for my talk at the crematorium arrived. For a while I spoke about how much Frank's family had loved him, how Ian, now in his thirties, would still rather go fishing with his dad than anyone else, and how much he would be missed by all his friends. It was all true. I didn't have to exaggerate or make anything up. Eventually I laid my notes down and looked directly at Ian and his mum as I spoke.

'I can't be sure what Frank thought about Jesus,' I said, 'but I'm sure of one thing. They'll have met by now. And I'd guess Jesus looked straight into his eyes and smiled, and said, "Frank, you brought love into someone's loveless world, you were a peacemaker, and you were a carpenter. I reckon we've got plenty to talk about."'

Were Frank and his wife unevenly yoked? Yes, thank the Lord. He was her unsigned gift from God. All the love that should have flowed from that horrible childhood and a godless church situation came into her life through him.

The crucial consideration in these matters? Only you and God know what is in your heart. Be honest with yourself and with him. Let Scripture guide you and offer advice. That's what it's there for. But whatever you do or don't do, never forget – God does what he wants.

So that's my stallion-sized hobby-horse – and, whatever you might say, it's a perfectly good metaphor!

Benny Hinn – or gin?

I don't want to get into chatter about specific personalities like Mr Hinn. If that's how he wants to wear his hair, it's up to him. With the 'terrified baby eaglet' hairstyle that I sport, who am I to judge? And white suits will become trendy again at some point in the next thousand years, so he needs to stay with that fashion choice.

But I definitely feel the need for strong drink when I watch some television evangelists, especially the ones who hawk the notion that giving them your cash is guaranteed to bring healing/breakthrough/freedom from addiction.

Frankly, I wish it was true. I can think of a few situations where I'd definitely flash my credit card and stretch my spending limit to the maximum.

What would it be worth to see my friend Anthony free of cancer, for my elderly mum to be clear-eyed again because the Goliath that is dementia had been tamed, or for the hi-def horror of ISIS executions to be brought to an end?

If the prayers of a Christian television celebrity could actually serve up those results, it would be worth organising a national whip-round to provide some funds to seal the deals.

But that's not how it works. You know it, I know it, and I suspect they know it too.

Besides, gin usually comes with tonic.

And a tonic is just what those results-for-cash faith pundits are not.

Should Christians laugh at rude jokes?

Probably not, but there are times when you just can't contain yourself. Awkward.

Those who follow Jesus don't have their capacity for seeing the funny side of lewd humour surgically removed. This can lead to huge embarrassment in social settings, especially when around Christians who do seem to have had their humour glands freeze-dried, or whose funny bones are broken beyond repair.

Perhaps you've been there. You're in the company of some people you're not too familiar with, and so you're initially cautious and reserved, not to mention clueless about their personal boundaries when it comes to funny stuff. When you don't know where the line is, it's easy to march clumsily right across it. Someone tells an epically amusing but somewhat salacious gag, and you desperately try *not* to laugh, because you're uncertain of the group, or because the joke or story has crossed your own personal line so you don't want to endorse the telling of it, but then, well, you just can't help it. You feel a rising wave of laughter rumbling inside you and, horrified, you desperately try to subdue those joyous reverberations, but without success. A widening smile grows into a stunted giggle, which morphs into a muffled guffaw. Then, finally surrendering, you just laugh out loud, howling away and slapping your thighs with gusto, only to look around at the rest of the group, whose wooden silence and architectural facial expressions show that they are appalled. They're offended, not just at the story that they found so terribly unfunny, but at *you*, for breaking step and finding it so hilarious. You then attempt to cover your own mirth, descend into loud coughing, or try to disguise your shaking shoulders as a symptom of an obscure medical condition.

It's even worse when you're the one telling the gag or 'funny' story, one which you deemed safe, but which is met with horror when you deliver the punchline. I did that once, and it really took me into a zone of shame that I don't ever want to revisit. It was actually one of Adrian's stories, so I blame him. The story still brings a smile to my lips every time I think of it. But the group I was with did not smile at all. They were mortified, as I soon was also at the appalled, blank silence that had so suddenly settled between us.

Of course, we do need to think a little about what constitutes 'rude'. Some Christians freak out at any mention of sex, whether it's mentioned in a serious teaching context or sprinkled with a little humour. The Bible is a lot more earthy and explicit about sex than most of us will ever be.

But while I don't want us to live lives constricted by religious corsets (now there's an unhelpful image), these days I tend to work to an 'if in doubt, don't bother' guideline. If the story is funny but questionable, at best it creates a smile or even a few seconds of laughter, but at worst it can seriously offend. In my view, the pay-off isn't worth the risk.

And speaking of corsets, I'm not an uptight Victorian – I never did understand their obsession with covering up table legs lest they become an object of ogling and lust. Personally, I've never found any furniture remotely alluring, despite owning a rather gorgeous coffee table. But it's not Victorian or narrow to say that dirty humour usually has the effect of leaving us feeling rather grubby. I do love it that Christians get to laugh out loud without having to be nudged into mirth by outright crudity, obscene language or downright filth ('downright filth' really does sound quite 'Dot Cotton', doesn't it?).

I'm saddened when I see genius mainstream comedians who are obviously so talented that they don't need to drop the 'F' bomb to get a response, and yet do. When they stoop to conquer in this way, rather than enhancing their talent, it diminishes them.

All that said, I'm so grateful that God invented laughter. Without it, life would be battleship grey. Apparently, some animals, like dogs and apes, have the capacity to laugh when tickled. And others don't. They're probably the ones that eat each other.

Is it all right for Christians to enjoy magic?

It is for me. I hope it is for you. I love watching magic. I always have done. The relationship between magician and audience is, at its best, such a cosy one. Magicians are transparently honest about their intention to deceive and amaze us. We, in our turn, want to be amazed and dazzled. How do they make things and people disappear? How can a cigarette pass easily through a solid coin? How does one object turn into another completely different object without ever leaving our sight? How can a man stand in mid-air, four inches above the pavement? How can that be?

'Trick us! Trick us!' we silently cry. 'Make us gasp in disbelief, and tease us with the notion that the illusion we have just witnessed is wondrously impossible. But don't tell us how you did it, even if we passionately beg you to explain. We want the sparkling magic. We certainly don't crave disclosure of the dull scaffolding that, we know in our hearts, must lie behind the false front.'

I love it all, I really do.

Of course, I am very aware that some Christians are darkly critical of performed magic. This is partly because they feel it smacks of the occult, that dark cavern we love to peer into even as we declare our horror to all and sundry, and partly because practitioners of the art are, by definition, telling lies to their audiences. I could waste half an hour or so disputing this patently illogical view, but I would prefer to offer a more positive perspective.

It becomes increasingly clear to me that a lot of the worldly enthusiasms and appetites displayed by human beings are indications of the healthy spiritual instincts that inevitably inhabit creatures made in the image of God.

Let's take doing the lottery as an example. Condemned by some as a temptation to descend into the twin pits of greed and gambling, this activity might actually be seen as an unconscious reaching out towards principles taught two thousand years ago by Jesus himself. People do the lottery because they want something wonderful to happen in their lives. They want the future to be transformed. They want to be very rich.

Jesus offers all of these things. Something wonderful happening in the lives of those who follow him, a transformed future, not just in this world but in the next, and riches beyond belief.

'Store up treasure in heaven,' he urges his listeners in the sixth chapter of Matthew's Gospel. The metaphors used by Jesus were always signposts to reality and truth. In some sense that is not easy to grasp in this distracting world, we need to open our account in heaven and organise direct debit payments. A warning. Don't tell anyone how wonderful you've been, or the money won't go through.

It's the same with magic. I believe there is an embedded understanding in the hearts of men and women that magic and miracle should be a part of authentic spirituality. Magicians take us a small but enjoyable distance along the path of that understanding, but Jesus takes us even further.

Imagine what it must have been like to hang around with the Son of God during those three years of street-preaching.

He needs money to pay a bill, so he tells his friend to go down to the lake, catch a fish and look inside its mouth. The bloke catches the fish, finds a coin in its mouth, and they use that money to settle his account. Brilliant!

He goes to a wedding and they run out of wine. He gets his beautiful assistants (the catering staff) to fill lots of big pots up with water. Next time they look in the pots, every drop of water has turned into wine – really good wine too. Stunning! How do you do that in the middle of a crowded wedding when everybody's watching?

It goes on and on. Walking on the surface of the water as if there was a bridge under his feet. Making a storm stop by shouting at it. Feeding five thousand people by breaking up a bit of bread and a few fish. Healing lepers. Making dead people come back to life. Letting himself be killed and buried, and then popping up alive and well a couple of days later. Wow! Unbelievable! All these things are simply spectacular.

Illusions? No. Tricks? No. Miracles? Yes. Wonderful illustrations of the fact that there is no clunky old scaffolding disappointingly shoring up the true acts of God. Not then, and not now. And there is, in the right sense, a touch of magic about it all, a resurgence of that sparkling excitement some of us were lucky enough to experience as small children when we woke in the early hours of Christmas morning and ran the tips of our quivering fingers over the intriguing shapes of gifts that Father Christmas had left for us.

Perhaps that is why C.S. Lewis insisted on Father Christmas appearing in Narnia. The wild things we claim to believe about Jesus far outweigh our childhood faith in flying reindeer and the logistically unlikely distribution of millions of presents by a jovial old fellow in a red coat, but I meet too many Christians who have lost the wonder and excitement and sheer magic of those childhood days. Sometimes, I am one of them.

I say we should rage against the death of wide-eyed wonder in the Church. Rage against boredom and thinly veiled secularism. Rage against an expectation that the scaffolding must always be revealed in the end. Gasp like a child at the miracles we see.

Enjoy the magic.

How do you respond to people who start their sentences with 'I'm only saying this in love'?

Usually I respond with one word.

'Really?'

And that's because of my experience with such loving truth-tellers to date.

I can't think of a single occasion when someone told me they were 'speaking the truth in love' and actually had much love about them. If you do truly speak in love, you don't seek to qualify it. And then again, if you don't speak in love, then you don't speak the truth at all, because your attitude taints the communication. That's why, when someone comes up to me and begins with that phrase, I usually don a crash helmet and head for the nearest nuclear shelter.

Christians are very good at using pious language to cover up our selfish inclinations. Usually what consumes us is what we like and don't like.

I feel troubled in my spirit. *I don't like this at all.*

We're not being fed. *I don't like your preaching much.*

The worship isn't anointed any more. *I don't like the songs we sing.*

We need to get back to the authentic Word of God. *I don't like the Bible translation we use.*

As the church gets bigger, we're losing our sense of family. *I don't like the kind of people who are showing up around here.*

I'm going to say this in love. *I don't like you.*

If the person uses piety to cover outright nastiness, I have to say I have much less tolerance these days.

Once I was having lunch with a church member who suddenly started making unspeakably insulting comments about me and my fellow leaders. I can't give details (first, because the comments were so offensive, and then because he might read this book, although I doubt it – he's not my greatest fan).

I got up and left.

And then there was the incident that stands in my memory as the greatest 'I say this in love' gaffe. I've written about it in several places elsewhere, but those books are out of print, and besides, it's worth repeating it.

A chap wandered up to me at the end of a wonderful service during a men's weekend. After delivering the standard 'I say this in love' disclaimer, he proceeded to tell me that he'd seen a mark on my forehead. I immediately started to rub my head, fearing that a little mascara had gone astray (I jest), or that I had slept awkwardly and got a friction burn on my head from the pillow (unlikely, but possible, I suppose). He interrupted my head-rubbing.

'No, I'm sorry to say that I think it might be . . . the mark of the beast.'

Right. Apparently I'm an Agent of Satan. What do you say to that? I decided to keep my mouth shut, not wanting to dignify this bizarre accusation with further dialogue. But I did ask him to go away.

You may disagree with me, but sometimes I think we Christians confuse meekness with allowing people to use us as a doormat. We pretend to be holier than thou when sticking the knife in, or sit there and take it when people insult us 'in love'. Jesus didn't hesitate to correct Peter bluntly when he spoke out of turn. Not that I'd make any comparisons between Jesus' ability to correct and my own skill in offering a mild rebuke, but sometimes bullies do need to be put firmly in their place.

Does drinking in social settings disqualify me from being a Christian?

Why on earth would it?

Jesus not only drank himself, but he laid on lashings of fine wine at a wedding, which was a very public setting indeed. He was also very popular as a party guest (and presumably not just because he was so gifted when it came to wine production). I know that some people, apparently irritated with our Lord about his Cana party piece, have tried to suggest that the wine was not alcoholic, which is rather silly, but not as absurd as the notion that when Paul told young Timothy to take a little wine to settle his squiffy tummy, he meant him to rub it on the outside of his belly . . .

There are some people who know they should never drink, because a sip allows the iron shackle of addiction to close around them. Equally, some Christians, rejoicing in the freedom to imbibe that is theirs, might need to imbibe a little less.

But the notion that enjoying a drink disqualifies us as believers is patently ridiculous.

Are the creative arts under-appreciated in the evangelical church?

Very much so, and especially in America, which seems surprising, as it's the home of Hollywood. Sometimes those who are obsessed with words and preaching ask me where creativity is to be found in the Bible. My retort is that it starts with the words, 'In the beginning, God created . . .' There's a clue for you.

Are you on Twitter?

No, I don't take drugs of any kind.

Some people in our prayer ministry team say that it is not God's will for any Spirit-filled believer to get ill. They say this to people who come to us for prayer. What would you say?

I'd say, 'Don't be silly.' And then, if they don't respond to that (which they usually don't), I'd say, 'Please go away.'

Christians get ill. Germs don't have religious scruples. And the statistics on death's success rate are rather impressive. One out of every one person dies.

So that kind of tosh just makes people who feel unwell feel worse. Before meeting the prayer ministry team, the sick person was just throwing up. Now, lashed with the ridiculous notion that they aren't holy/prayerful/filled with faith enough, they feel bad about their hearts and souls as well as their bodies. Some of these slogan-toting prayer ministry people could get a job working for Job . . . get it?

If you help someone when you're grumpy, does it count? I know God loves cheerful givers, but sometimes I'm not cheerful but a bit grumpy.

Perhaps you're feeling grumpy because it's costing you a lot, or you're concerned that your sacrifice is not being appreciated by the person who is on the receiving end. Either way, I think it counts more.

**TELLING IT LIKE
IT REALLY IS . . .**

We've had so many storms hitting our lives lately. What do you and your wife do when that happens to you?

I suppose you want the truthful answer to that question, don't you? A shame. So much easier to make a nice list of biblical principles that sound all right, even if they don't really work the way they're supposed to. And I might be able to supply that list for you if it wasn't for the fact that the last year of our lives has turned out to be one of the most storm-filled periods we have ever known.

Real life. Such a bugger, isn't it? Someone said to me on the phone the other day (probably quoting the book of James) that one positive aspect of life's problems is that they do help to build character.

After a brief pause I said, with remarkable Christian restraint, 'I think Bridget and I would say that our characters have been built quite sufficiently for the time being, thank you very much. We'd quite like a couple of nice, trouble-free months to give us a chance to discover if this last stage of character building is likely to be sufficient to carry us through the next immensely valuable, rubbish-strewn phase of our lives.'

All right, I will try to tell you exactly what helps us, and if you can pick any meat off the bones for yourself, you're very welcome.

First, we have each other. A huge benefit. Someone to hold your hand when the thunder and lightning is over-whelming. Someone who will huddle in a damp corner of the boat with you when hope is draining away at a terri-fying rate. Someone who, when the storm has abated, will keep the secret of just how much you both fell apart when the paucity of your resources was revealed. All of that and much more. We are very lucky to be in possession of such riches.

We are fortunate, blessed if you like, to have enough and to spare, so we do try to offer a haven to anyone who needs to join us at sea. After all, people have done it for us in the past. Which brings me to something else that helps to bring us through the storms.

Family and friends.

We love them all. They are so precious to us.

Jesus seems to have felt the same, but his closest companions were a bit disappointing sometimes, weren't they? I am drawn back again and again to the Gospel accounts of Jesus agonising in the garden of Gethsemane. There is something so ghastly and wonderful about his intensely human struggle to achieve enough peace to cope with the horror that was to come. Clearly, he did not want to go through the physical, spiritual and emotional pain that was beckoning. He was deeply distressed, to the point of feeling crushed.

'You can do anything. Please, if it's possible, tell me I

54

don't have to do this,' he begged his Father, 'That's what I'd like. But above all I want to be obedient to you.'

He'd parked his three friends, Peter, James and John, a few yards away, drawing support from the fact that (theoretically) they were watching and praying as he clung onto his determination to be faithful while he navigated through an unimaginably violent storm of fear and distress. Those three fellows didn't do so well, did they? Three times Jesus discovered them stretched out on the grass under the trees, willing spirits surrendered to weary flesh, simply unable to keep their tired eyes propped open.

The Bible still tends to be read aloud in a steady voice, ironing out any extremes of emotion, as though granular revelation is somehow shameful. Because of this it is hard for us to imagine the hurt and disappointment in the Master's voice as he addressed Simon Peter after finding him asleep on the first occasion.

'Simon, are you asleep? Couldn't you keep watch for one hour?'

I suppose the disciples were not very accustomed to Jesus displaying such vulnerability. When the pillars that hold up our existence start to creak and crack, we get very uneasy. The roof might cave in. There is something ineffably plaintive about the disciples' reaction, or lack of reaction, to being found slumbering yet again.

They did not know what to say to him. (Mark 14:37, 40)

Well, of course they didn't.

I can't help feeling just a bit sorry for them. It had been a very long day and they had no real understanding of what was happening. How could they know that he was in the process of finalising an agonising decision that would save the world? What they did know was that they had let their master down. Jesus was clearly in profound distress. He needed his friends and they had not been able to stay awake, even for sixty minutes.

One of the helpful lessons this story might teach us is that getting through a storm is not just about relying on abstract divine support. Jesus loved and depended on his Father, but that night he needed his friends. Flesh and blood, close, attentive, and preferably awake. We need to use our friends. If they really are our friends, they will want to help. They may even be willing to sit in the darkness with us. And they are not mere substitutes for God. They are his special gifts to us – even if they do fall asleep sometimes.

It is so easy to undervalue the good things that support us through the wild times. So easy to regard our small but ever-present aids to peace as trivial items in comparison with what we regard as spiritually significant gifts from God.

I think the time has come to mention TEA.

People sometimes say, 'It's just a storm in a teacup.' This usually means that a problem or difficulty that has little scope for causing real damage is being taken far too seriously. I understand this, but Bridget and I would like to share with you another way to look at this whole storm and teacup scenario. Over the last few months we have often found sleep difficult as we wrestle with problems and worries that seem totally insoluble at three o'clock in the morning. Because of this we have cultivated the habit of ensuring that everything needed for the making of tea is ready for action at any time of the night.

I'm sure many will be familiar with a particular and time-honoured dialogue that occasionally punctuates the dismal dark. It usually occurs when one of us has become aware that, for several minutes, neither of us has been making any night noises.

'Are you awake?'

'Yes, are you?'

(Stupid question!)

'Yes.'

'Shall we have a cup of tea?'

(Another stupid question!)

'Yes!'

Light clicks on. Kettle makes slow, sweet journey-to-boiling noises. Cups and spoons clatter and clink. Kettle begins its little two-hundred-and-twelve-degree-Fahrenheit bubbling praise party. Water is poured. Milk is added – oh, so delicately. A packet rustles and rips as stubborn biscuits are levered from their hiding place. The first sip is imminent. It is taken. Surprised by such unexpected joy, the devil retreats, angry and baffled yet again by the power of his enemy's small but perfectly formed creations.

The point is that, however huge and unmanageable the storm might be, you simply cannot fit it into a teacup – not when that teacup is filled with tea. For a few minutes in the middle of the night, tea rules supreme, and a fresh perspective means that a little more precious sleep might at least be possible. Yes, of course, dear pedants, we all like different drinks, varieties of tea and ways of preparing it (in the middle of the night in the bedroom there may be up to fifty shades of Earl Grey), but the principle remains the same. A little of what relaxes you does you good, and as far as Bridget and I are concerned, tea always steps up to the plate – or saucer.

If Peter, James and John had been equipped with a primus stove, a box of Yorkshire teabags and a small carton of long-life milk it might have been a better night for all concerned. We are more fortunate than them. We have tea. Thank God for the little things that make a difference. He made them, and he must be very proud.

Finally, a brief mention of one more thing we have found useful when the winds are howling and the clouds are rolling in. This may not seem a great plan on the face of it, but often it really can bring relief. Ask God to give you a job to do. In tackling that task, if he is kind or cruel enough to give you one, you may well find more genuine comfort than in many abstract, so-called spiritual exercises.

To anyone and everyone reading this, I wish you well as you tackle your own storms. Whatever your personal list of God-given storm aids – meditation, salvation, bacon sandwiches, Bible verses or having your hair brushed – may you find comfort in the moment, and still waters and blue skies at the end of the journey.

What is the most significant thing that you have learned in the last decade?

Wow. Big question. A few years ago, I think I might have heard that question as, 'What's the most significant thing that God has told you?' – but I'm glad you phrased the question as you did, asking me about lessons learned. There have been plenty.

Let me be clear. God *does* speak today. He's not mute, distant, uninterested – shrugging his shoulders and challenging the universe, 'Am I bovvered?' But I do think that he's quieter than some of us make him out to be. I feel a mixture of emotions when in the presence of those breathlessly enthusiastic believers with whom God is so *very* chatty. They paint God as an endless natterer, who is constantly updating them about minor details like what tie they should wear with that blue shirt, where they should park their car and whether lamb would be better than beef for Sunday lunch, and all of this chatter shared while he continues to oversee everything everywhere and carry on billions of other simultaneous conversations, which is rather splendid multi-tasking, even for God. I can't decide whether to be quite intimidated by these people with whom God is so conversational, or encourage them to book in for a chat with a therapist.

God *does* speak to me (not as often as I'd like), but of late the manner of his speaking has tended to be through lessons learned and conclusions drawn, rather than a subjective feeling, a stonking prophecy or a vivid dream in the night. Coming from the charismatic wing of the Church, I'm convinced that our crowd talks too much about *revelation* – God speaking – and not enough about *wisdom* – our learning, not just the lessons of life, but more about the nature and heart of God, as we journey through our days, and making notes to self as we do so.

OK, enough of that little detour about how God speaks. Back to the question.

The biggest lesson of my last decade, one that I so wish I had learned forty years ago, is this:

Everything is broken.

This fact has made such an impact on me that I have spoken about it endlessly in public and private, and written about it elsewhere too. But it bears repeating.

Everything is broken.

There's nothing that is without cracks, flaws and fault lines. Every organisation, church, marriage, person, project, you, me – it's all, we're all, broken. And the sooner I face that fact, the happier I'll be.

'Cynic!' I hear some cry, insisting that I've become jaded as the years have passed, that I've lost my virginal sense of hopefulness. Others will fear that I'm settling for compromise as I insist that no matter how hard we work, how much in love we might be, however fantastic that local church is, it's all broken. But I'm not succumbing to cynicism, and I'm certainly not running up the white flag, surrendering to everything being mediocre and second best.

I'm just adjusting my sights and realigning myself to a more authentic hope, one that I think is reflective of what Scripture tells us about the human condition.

As a passionate new Christian, I believed our local church was so brilliant that if we could just persuade the BBC to bring their cameras in on a Sunday morning, the whole nation would be immediately saved. Forty years later, I've seen the church at its best and at its worst. It is loaded with self-sacrificing volunteers, quietly heroic souls who are taking communion on Sundays and undergoing chemotherapy on Mondays, and elderly ladies who go out on the streets of our cities every Saturday night to be surrogate grandmas to hopelessly inebriated teenagers. And I've seen critical, petty, carping souls who fight about song choices and Bible translations and someone taking their beloved pew (which is not theirs). I've met Christians who talk about the joy of the Lord but who are well-practised miseries – would-be Olympic champions, if it were possible to win a gold medal for snivelling.

This side of forever, we won't see straight, or be fully straight. There are many hints and touches of the kingdom of God about, but all will only be complete on that great and glorious day when that kingdom will be fully inaugurated and finally established.

In the meantime, we live in the mean times. Knowing that everything is broken means that we don't have to be shattered by disappointment, stalked by disillusionment, or bewildered when our idealistic expectations aren't met. We may be saddened when that vintage marriage breaks down, when that man who seemed so very upright, the soul of consistency, abandons his bride of five decades for a newer, younger version, but we won't be fundamentally surprised, because we have no illusions about human nature. And we'll be less likely to walk away from the church muttering that it's a house of hypocrites, which is an unjust slur, seeing as we are the ones who openly declare that we're sinners in need of ongoing grace.

I left one denomination partly because I was indignant that it was broken, and went off and joined the new church movement, which was also broken. The church I serve now is growing, imaginative, flourishing, and broken. But I have no criticism here: I contribute to the flaws of everything that I am a part of, because I bring my own brokenness into the mix whenever I show up.

Helpfully for us, God only uses fragile, broken, under-construction people. Don't believe the myths propagated by the endlessly sleek, we've-got-it-together souls. Beneath the surface and the sheen, there are always hairline cracks. That's how God gets in.

Do parts of the Bible ever make you cry?

An unusual and interesting question. Yes, they do. There's quite a list, but I've chosen four examples to tell you about.

One is that moment in the eighteenth chapter of the second book of Samuel when King David learns that his son Absalom has been killed when the mule he is riding passes beneath a tree and he is caught by the hair in its branches. Only later does he discover that the young man was actually killed by Joab, the king's commander of forces, who thrust three darts into his heart as he hung helplessly from the tree. David is all too aware that his conflict with Absalom is a part of the punishment that God has decreed as a consequence of his adultery with Bathsheba and his callous murder of her husband Uriah. He is apparently able to accept this judgement of God, but as all we parents who have made mistakes with our children know, the pain of witnessing the results of our messing up is almost unbearable.

'O my son Absalom! My son, my son Absalom! If only I had died instead of you – O Absalom, my son, my son!' (verse 33)

David's unrestrained grief is a gross offence to Joab, the commander of his army, and to the men who have fought and died on behalf of the king. As far as they are concerned he loves those who hate him and hates those who love him. This is completely understandable, and I completely understand it. But I am also a father, and I know how it feels to choke with sorrow over tragedy in the lives of my children. God and I, both.

A second sad little spot comes in Leviticus. Most of you are, of course, accomplished theologians, and will know this book more or less by heart. So you will readily understand that these twenty-seven chapters do not offer an emotional rollercoaster of an experience, except perhaps for those who enjoy rollercoasters that travel very, very, very slowly down gentle little slopes with the brakes on.

Nevertheless, there is a sentence of only three words in the tenth chapter that brought a tear to my eye when I first read it in context. It concerns Aaron, the hapless brother and temporary mouthpiece of Moses, shortly after his two sons had become priests and the entire company had, with great joy, seen fire come out from the presence of the Lord to consume the burnt offering.

The two young men, Nadab and Abihu, then took it upon themselves to offer their own, unauthorised fire to the Lord (there's a lot of it about in this age), and the Lord, to put it mildly, was not pleased. Fire came out from the presence of God once more, but this time it consumed Nadab and Abihu. The two brothers, still dressed in the charred remains of outfits that must have made them look like a cross between Dame Edna Everage and Widow Twanky, were dead. And their father, seeing his dreams destroyed and lying at his feet – what did he say?

All the Bible tells us is this: 'Aaron remained silent.'

So sad, don't you think?

Before you begin to get the idea that I am fixated on emotional father-son dramas (perish the thought), let me move on to my third tear-inducing moment. This one is encapsulated in just two words, possibly one of the most famous verses in the Bible.

'Jesus wept.'

I have already written a great deal on this subject in the past, but I cannot answer this question without expressing my profound feeling for Jesus as he felt himself emotionally torn apart by the immediate demands of his friends Martha, Mary and Lazarus on one side and his absolute commitment to the will of his Father on the other. A full-frontal attack from Martha followed by the weeping collapse of her sister Mary must have rocked him from head to toe.

'If you had been here, my brother would not have died.'
Jesus was shredded. No wonder he wept.

If he wept, and if we weep for him, then perhaps we should also weep for ourselves. If we are seriously intending to follow Jesus and to obey the will of God in our lives, we are likely to experience our own agonising conflicts. There may well be times when the decisions we make are unpopular and unacceptable to those who feel they have a claim on us. They may give us a hard time.

Just one set of clothes and a pair of sandals. No bread, no bag, no money in your belt, no extra tunic – no compromise, no soft options. Life on the road can be very tough.

Yes, we might weep.

One more. It's Jesus again. Here are the verses. They come from the end of the sixth chapter of John's Gospel.

From this time many of his disciples turned back and no longer followed him.

'You do not want to leave too, do you?' Jesus asked the Twelve.

Simon Peter answered him, 'Lord, to whom shall we go? You have the words of eternal life. We have come to believe and to know that you are the Holy One of God.' (verses 66–69)

Did Jesus know that he would get this response from Peter? He might have done, but the Gospels make it very clear that the Son of God did not have advance knowledge of all things. He seems to have been spontaneously shocked, amazed, angered and delighted in a number of situations, especially those where individuals demonstrated extremes of doubt or faith. Perhaps, on this occasion, his spirits dipped in a very normal, human way as the majority of his followers disappeared and he was faced with the possibility that even the twelve disciples he had originally chosen might turn their backs on him.

But, as we know, they didn't, and how warmly reassuring that little speech of Peter's must have been. As a matter of fact, Bridget and I find ourselves echoing his words again and again when times get tough and it becomes increasingly easy to see why the road less travelled is actually less travelled.

When bad stuff happens, it may be that, like us, you are sometimes tempted to turn away – but where would we go? That's the problem. He does indeed have the words of eternal life, and hope – the secret of the triumph of love. Those are the things we want more than anything, aren't they? So we decide to stick with him in the end, and we're always glad we have. If it cheers him up as well, that's a bonus.

Do you ever say things in public that you later regret in private?

Occasionally, though not as much as I used to. That's not because I am massively cleverer and wiser than previously; it's because I have learned that I have an enormous capacity for inserting foot firmly in mouth, and so am a little more hesitant to make off-the-cuff comments that are not thought through. And I genuinely fear hurting people with a 'clever' quip that might get a cheap laugh but could cut someone to the quick. If anyone is going to be the butt of fun or the victim in my stories, it needs to be me. Or the devil. But mostly me.

When I was in Bible college, we had preaching classes, and one of the lecturers was teaching on what we should do if we felt that we had made an erroneous or insensitive comment while preaching. He said (if I heard him rightly) that we should just move on. Stopping to correct the mistake, or apologising for words spoken in haste, would just draw attention to the error, said he. I think that was poor advice.

There have been a few times when I have felt that the tone, rather than the content, of what I have said was harsh or even bullying. Sadly, that's happened on some occasions when I was preaching to crowds of multiple thousands, so my error was more obvious for all to see. Coming to the end of the sermon, I've known from the niggling sense of internal discomfort that I was harsh. When that has happened, I've ended the talk, prayed, and then asked the congregation for a moment more of their time – and then, pointing out my error, I've apologised. Ironically, on the occasions that this has happened, it felt like my credibility went up with the congregation because of the acknowledgement of this error, rather than down because of my tone or rash words. But whatever the result, the principle is this: bullying leaders shouldn't be tolerated. If we get it wrong, we should apologise.

Sometimes speaking across different cultures complicates things (and it makes humour challenging, as I've mentioned before) but there's really no excuse for the horrifying tale I'm about to tell you. In America the term 'retarded' is still in fairly common use, as is the word 'handicapped'. Sometimes people use the word 'retard' in an extremely unkind way to describe someone who is foolish, idiotic or (horribly) has learning difficulties. And the phrase 'totally retarded' is sometimes used to ridicule a ridiculous idea or attitude. I'm not defending the use of these terms, just stating a fact.

I had flown back from the USA and was speaking in the Big Top at Spring Harvest, and a combination of jetlag and just my own homegrown stupidity meant that I used the term 'totally retarded' to describe an idea that I thought was silly.

At the end of the meeting, I was confronted by a furious lady, incensed that I had used this insensitive language. She was quite right to be so frustrated, because this was not just an issue of using politically incorrect vocabulary – my carelessness had created a sense of exclusion. Her frustration was fuelled by the fact that she had worked tirelessly to bring a group of people to the event, each of whom had learning difficulties, only to hear the Reverend Clod (that would be me) use such a bruising phrase during the evening. Tearfully, I apologised, and was eventually forgiven, but I could see how irate she was. I have no words of condemnation for her anger. How I wish I had engaged brain before opening mouth that night. It happened years ago now, but I deeply regret it still.

What is your greatest achievement?

Taking risks of faith. When we were living in America, we made a decision to launch out into an itinerant ministry solely supported by the churches that we would serve. We had a low bank balance, a relatively empty schedule and no donors lined up to take up the slack, but we felt that it was what God was asking us to do, and that he would take care of us.

We made a similar tough decision nearly four years later when we sensed that we should come back to the UK. At that time we had a promise of just a few thousand pounds per year from the church that was offering to be our base and, unlike the USA, you can't just call up UK churches and ask to be invited to speak. I can still remember the feeling of rising panic as the airplane taxied down the runway and I wondered, as we left the USA, what would become of us. We had no permanent place to live – a couple in the church were travelling for six months and had offered us their apartment for rent on a temporary basis, but we had no idea where we would find a roof for our heads for the long term. But again, God stepped in – in ways that were remarkable.

Are you frightened by any fruits?

That is a very personal, profound question, and I intend to give it serious consideration.

OK. I've given it several buckets of deep thought, and here is the outcome.

I do have a longstanding problem with tomatoes.

There, I've said it. I never thought I would.

And if we are being truly honest, there are scars from wounds caused by betrayal and disappointment experienced in orange, satsuma and tangerine contexts.

The tomato issue is complex and multifaceted. I have used tomato ketchup for as long as I can remember, in fact one of my favourite rhyming couplets as a child was this one:

> Shake, oh shake the ketchup bottle,
> First none'll come, and then a lot'll.

The thing you have to understand, though, is that my innocent, childish mind never made the connection between actual tomatoes and the ketchup that was made from them. Tomatoes were tomatoes. Ketchup was ketchup.

Life was so much simpler then. As a matter of interest (and I know you are riveted with interest), it wouldn't

70

have mattered in those early days if I had seen the connection. The tomatoes grown in our greenhouse were sweet, good-natured little creatures with a distinct tomato flavour. I loved them. And yes, I ate them. For, as I vaguely recall Oscar Wilde putting it, 'Yet each man eats the fruit he loves . . .'

As the years passed my liking for ketchup continued, but a pall of darkness was slowly enveloping my relationship with tomatoes themselves. Those gentle, balmy, far-off greenhouse days were gone for ever, and the things that continued to brazenly masquerade as tomatoes were not as in former times. They were sour. They were either gruesomely squishy or jeeringly resistant to the penetration of human teeth. Some were ridiculously big. They tasted of nothing and seemed mindlessly unaware of that deficiency. They refused to mix freely with the rest of the salad – too proud, one suspects, to be associated with the colour green. There is surely no uglier manifestation of racism than salad discrimination.

I became an abstainer, and remain so to this day (other than in cheese and tomato sandwiches, which I really like, and ketchup, as I've already mentioned, and also tomato soup, my favourite soup of all, and tomato relish, which is good for dipping – oh, and I nearly forgot, sundried tomatoes, which are great with olives).

Those who do not share my belief in God might be interested to know that, since finishing the previous paragraph, I have spoken on the phone to my friend Peter Ryder, who, on hearing that I was writing about tomatoes, told me the story of his own Damascus Road experience in this context. Peter's revelation did not happen precisely on the Damascus Road, you understand. It was actually on the road to Pocklington, a small market town at the foot of the Yorkshire Wolds, but the effect was similar. Peter stopped in a layby to eat a sandwich that had been prepared for him by his wife. As he bit into it he entered into what he describes as a dual reality. He found himself eating pieces of tomato, a fruit or berry that hitherto had been anathema to him. At the same instant he realised that he was not only eating but *enjoying* the food that he had vowed would never pass his lips again.

Life was never the same after that. Peter stopped kicking against the goads and gave himself over to tomatoes, especially in the south of France. Was that God, or was that God?

The orange thing is largely my wife's fault, I'm sorry to say. We have been married for forty-four years, and an otherwise happy relationship has been soured only by her inexplicable determination to feed me oranges, satsumas and tangerines that are simply not sweet enough to eat. I end up believing her seductive lies every time – every single time.

'Come on, just have a little bit of this orange. You'll love it. It's really juicy and sweet.'

'That's what you said the last time, and it wasn't. It was sour and I hated it.'

'Yes, but this one's different. I tell you – this one's almost too sweet for *me* to eat.'

'No, I don't think I'll . . .'

'Oh, go on, just one little teensy-weensy segment. Just pop it in your mouth.'

'Oh, all right, go on then . . .'

'Tell me what you think.'

'Aargh!'

Inedible as usual. Had to spit it out as usual. Betrayed and misled as usual. Mind you, I shouldn't be surprised. This is a woman who eats grapefruit halves for pleasure. Without sugar! (I only learned about this after we recited our vows before God and the vicar. Grounds for annulment, some might say.) She made all those promises, but never thought to mention that a variety of citrus fruits would ever stand between us.

Ah well, we have had it out, and there are compensations. My wife and I are agreed on one thing. He is the vine and we are the branches. And any branch that does not bear fruit gets cut off and burned. So we have agreed that Bridget will do the spiritual equivalent of tomatoes, oranges and all other citrus fruits, and I'll do bananas, ripe pears, strawberries and other sweet, unaggressive items. So far, it seems to be working.

By the way, many thanks are due to the person who asked this question. Intellectually and spiritually, you have significantly raised the bar.

If you could invent your own Christian denomination, what would it be like and what would you call it?

I wouldn't bother. There are already so many denominations, and the last thing the world needs is another one. Some sources suggest that there are between 30,000 and 40,000 denominations around the world right now. While not all of those differentiate themselves based on what they believe (some of them are simply national organisations or independent groupings), it's still amazing how many people have at some point insisted that they are more right than everybody else, to the extent that they have felt compelled to start an organisation around the unique shape of their correctness.

But with that in mind, a coalition of groups, networks and denominations that were formerly independent or even hostile to each other, working together cooperatively and mingling diversity with respect – now that would be something I'd love to be part of. If nothing else, it would reduce the number of denominations that exist rather than increase it.

What would I call this new coalition? Perhaps the word 'united' would be in the title. Or perhaps not. That's been done.

Who irritates you?

Too many people, I am sad to say. If I had to choose one in particular right now I think I'd have to pick on Katie Hopkins, the *Sun* columnist, an acid-tongued, poison-penned pundit who freely critiques everyone and everything. She's cruel, impossibly bigoted and seems to think that she represents popular opinion, verbalising what many hesitate to say but actually feel. If she does, and if it's true that most people really do think like her, then I'm moving to Mars. Recently she pledged to move away from Britain if a particular political party came to power, which probably helped that party win more votes. She tears into people who are overweight, disabled and unemployed; she rails at children who have 'common' names, an epithet that just means names she doesn't like; and she even rants about refugees fleeing for asylum, boasting that she'd deal with them with a gunship. I pray for her, (a) that she will shut up, or (b) that she will find Jesus, and then either shut up or say something nice.

But there is another irritating soul who makes me bristle. When I think about Katie Hopkins, I become like Katie Hopkins: I have thoughts about her that are cruel and bigoted, and I rail and rant – evidence of this is presented in the previous paragraph. And I also told you in that same paragraph that I pray for her, which is the Christian thing to say, but I don't, and I should.

So, who irritates me most? Me.

**THAT'S A
TRICKY ONE!**

JEFF

If you were only allowed one more prayer, what would it be?

I so want to be frivolous with this one, but I can't. Every time I try to find something witty to say in response, two images come to mind.

The first is of those drug smugglers shot by firing squad in Indonesia some months ago. Numbers of them (perhaps all) had become followers of Jesus, and it's reported that they sang to him as they were led to the place where they were shot. And the other image is of those twenty or so Coptic Christians who were forced to their knees on a sunny beach by some digitally blurred ISIS thugs, and then decapitated. It's said that they sang too.

So perhaps my one remaining prayer would be phrased as a song.

But what would the lyrics be? Would it be a simple sentence of thanksgiving, or a prayer for blessing for my lovely family, or a last attempt at repentance for my shortcomings?

In pondering this, my thoughts turned to Jesus and his last prayer. 'Father, into your hands I commit my spirit.'

What better prayer could be prayed, at the last moment or at any moment?

It affirms my belief about who God is, and how I am called to relate to him. Father. Not just any old father. Jesus never taught that God is like your actual dad, which is a relief to those who tragically suffered at the hands of the one man they thought they could utterly trust. Rather, he taught that God is like no father we've ever known, that he is quite unlike earthly fathers, who, even at their best, are evil in the sense that they are still marred and flawed by sin.

And then, 'Into your hands I commit my spirit.'

In other words, I've done what I can, and now it's over to you, God. Of course, in Jesus' case, he was able to say that he had done everything he had been sent to do. In your case and mine, we'd be saying that we've done what we could, but sometimes, regretfully, we did not do all we could. But now it's over to you, not just to an impersonal God, but our Father. You're trustworthy. Your hands are well-worn, faithful. I can succumb now to whatever is ahead: be it life, be it death, I'm falling into your arms.

Perhaps that's what those men in orange jumpsuits on a sunny, hellish beach, or those retired drug smugglers in Indonesia, were saying in their songs. Over to you, God.

How can I find my way safely through the minefield of different doctrines and ideas in Christianity?

There is, of course, nothing remotely funny about real minefields, but the use of that particular metaphor in this question did bring a smile to my face. The idea that actual engagement with any particular doctrine or idea would invariably result in spiritual destruction might be just a tad pessimistic. Perhaps the questioner was implying that there are certain spiritually sophisticated mines that explode in a benevolent sort of way. Maybe there is some truth in that.

Nonetheless, I do know exactly what he or she is getting at. Politics and religion are alike in the sense that they are very far from being exact sciences, although plenty of people are convinced that they ought to be. Therefore there is almost invariably a hectoring quality to the style of presentation used by those who wish to promote a view that cannot be supported with anything so mundane as facts and evidence.

I must say, I think I have encountered almost every sub-variety of such a style. There is shouting. There is heavy emphasis, accompanied by lengthy meaningful pauses. There is a strange, soupy manner, delivered with a moist and humourless smile that always makes me want to run out of the church and commit a nice obvious sin somewhere. There is the Dutch auction style of evangelism, in which the speaker adjusts the price of salvation downwards to progressively lower levels until the members of his audience are balanced on the edge of their seats like greyhounds frantically straining to burst from their traps. There are those who operate as though the Holy Spirit is contained in a sort of header tank somewhere up in the attic of their heads. Every now and then these speakers have to pause meaningfully as they run out of spiritual force and need to wait for a top-up.

I could go on, but I'm enjoying myself too much. I would just like to mention the way in which Jesus went about communicating faith. I have to warn you that he was lamentably lacking in good solid doctrine when it came to addressing ordinary people, but it might be worth just glancing at his preferred method.

He told stories. Short parables that use familiar situations to make a moral or religious point. He created an imaginative space in which those who listened could move around freely, look at options and consider for themselves the very best place to land with their thinking. People not only enjoyed the stories Jesus told, they were fed by the fruit that grew from those narrative vines.

How much of the ministry of Jesus consisted of parables? A little bit? Ten per cent? Twenty? Here is a clue from the thirteenth chapter of Matthew's Gospel (verses 34–35):

Jesus spoke all of these things to the crowd in parables; he did not say anything to them without using a parable. So was fulfilled what was spoken through the prophet:

'I will open my mouth in parables,
   I will utter things hidden since the creation of
the world.'

Jesus also said that he wanted his listeners to count the cost carefully before taking a step in the direction of following him. In other words, his aim was not to court mindless agreement, but to foster healthy decision-making. I believe that genuine ministry of the Holy Spirit never shuts us down. It opens us up to new possibilities and ways of thinking. It allows us to recognise and own the real changes that happen in us. It is the product of a creative spirit, a spirit that enjoys story and loves to see movement and delight in those who hear it.

Doesn't sound much like a minefield, does it?

Somebody told me that, at their church, God has been giving people gold fillings in their teeth during the services. What do you think?

I'm confused by it all. Sorry, but I simply don't under-stand why God would want to give anyone gold fillings in their teeth, unless he was trying to bless a dentally enthusiastic rapper for whom flashing a gleaming set of golden molars is a fashion statement. God designed teeth to be made out of enamel and dentin. So why not just give people new teeth, rather than gold bits? It seems a little like God giving a person in a wheelchair a new set of tyres . . .

Is your son Gerald in the *Sacred Diaries* based on a real person?

If I had a pound for every time I've been asked this question over the last thirty years, I would be able to pay for one of David Beckham's haircuts. The answer, as always, is yes and no. Yes, he was based on a real person, and the real person was me. When I wrote the first *Sacred Diary* I needed to include a free spirit who could say all the (relatively) outrageous things that were on my mind. Creating seventeen-year-old Gerald solved that problem. Gerald's engagingly unfettered approach to life enabled me to crack open a few windows that were rusted from disuse, and allow some fresh air into a Christian world that seemed very stuffy to me at the time.

My beloved oldest son, Matthew, was twelve when the first *Diary* was published in 1987, and although he became significantly more Geraldish as the years passed, he was definitely not the original inspiration for my fictional offspring. Matt did get pretty fed up with people asking him if Gerald was his alter ego, to the extent that some enterprising person sent him a t-shirt printed on the front with the words 'CALL ME MATTHEW BECAUSE . . .' and on the back with 'MY NAME IS NOT GERALD'. I don't think he wore it very often. Not surprising, really, when you consider the bewilderment that was likely to be caused by such an odd and superfluous message in any context outside the tiny world of Christian books.

One more interesting aspect of my imaginary son was the fact that quite a lot of teenage girls were keen to know if he had a girlfriend. Gerald could have had a very active social life, if only he had been sensible enough to exist.

The latest *Sacred Diary*, a book in which 'Adrian' is charged with organising a church weekend away, introduces us to Gerald's wife Josie and their teenage son Cameron, a young man who takes his father's wackiness to new heights – or depths, depending on how you look at it.

So – sorry, girls, it's too late. Anyway, you've grown up and got your own kids by now, probably. It's fair enough, though. Josie doesn't exist either. They're well suited.

What is the best pub that you have ever visited?

I love my local, The Bridge at Amberley. Harvey's Sussex Best (the nectar of heaven) is on tap, the food is good, but more importantly it's a place of real welcome. I live just a hundred yards from another pub, but I avoid it, because although the food is excellent, the atmosphere is usually lukewarm (and occasionally downright chilly). When I go to The Bridge, I'm often welcomed by name. Dave and Tash, who run the pub, work especially hard at building a real sense of community. It's everything that a local pub should be, and it recently won West Sussex Pub of the Year. The award was well deserved.

Mind you, I did have a rather embarrassing experience in The Bridge. I got chatting with a local and told him where I lived, which is an apartment in a large manor house in a village nearby.

'I've heard that there's a bloke who's moved in there who spends a lot of time in America,' he ventured. 'Apparently he's a bit famous in the world that he works in, writes books, but nobody knows much about him and his wife. Do you know him?'

I wondered how to respond, and finally confessed that he might just possibly be referring to me, which was a bit awkward, seeing as he had tagged me as being 'a bit famous'. Some people know my name because of my speaking and writing, but it's the Christian world, so fame there is not so much like being a little fish in a big pond, it's more like being a tiny tiddler of a goldfish in one of those plastic bags you sometimes see at the fairground.

His face flushed red, and he simply said, 'Oh shit!'

Jeff, what are some of the challenges of Christian leadership for you personally?

I hesitate to respond to this, simply because I feel so privileged to do what I do. Just today someone kindly texted me, commenting that it must be wonderful to be able to bring hope, joy and faith to people, and although it often surprises me that this happens through my flawed efforts, they are absolutely right. It is rather wonderful. And life has been an amazing adventure – I've been blessed to travel the world and meet some stunning people. In many ways, I have absolutely nothing to complain about.

I occasionally have to go into central London to record radio shows. When I clamber into a packed tube train, and stare into the armpits of a stranger in sweltering heat, in a cattle-truck crush that is surely a health-and-safety nightmare, I remember my own days of commuting into the city for two hours every day. I realise that most of these people endure this bovine experience daily, and some of them will do it for four decades of their lives. And those are the ones who are lucky enough to have a job. So to be clear, any niggles that I have should be seen in that context.

But since you asked, I will mention just a couple of the challenges.

In common with every other Christian leader, I invest in the invisible. Occasionally I envy those who can end their week saying that they've helped assemble a thousand cars, reached their sales target, or arranged eleven mortgages. They have tangible, measurable results to show for their labours. I spend quite a lot of time preaching, an activity that, as Jesus said, is a bit like taking sackloads of seed and then tossing it everywhere, hoping that the seeds will settle, take root and eventually produce some fruit. You hope that somebody will be helped, that another person might be nudged towards faith. But even when somebody shows an outward response, coming forward at the end of a service for prayer, raising a hand to acknowledge their desire to act on what they've heard, there's no guarantee that good decisions made in that moment will stick. And anyone in Christian leadership knows the grief that comes when you've invested much in someone, only to have them turn their back on God, on you, or both.

That's one reason why I have to be very careful in asking people to respond at the end of a sermon, because I'm not always sure whether those appeals or so-called altar calls are for the listeners, or for the personal endorsement of the preacher, who is desperate for a self-vindicatory 'result'. So working with the intangible and the invisible can be difficult at times.

Do you find the concept of the Trinity hard to explain?

Quite impossible. All those analogies of fire, ice and water, or three-leaf clover, don't help me much either. Some elements of the Christian faith frankly baffle me, and the Trinity is one of them. Another is the thought of Jesus, the eternal Son of God who has always been, morphing into a tiny speck in a young virgin's womb. Getting one's head around that idea is surely impossible. But without sounding blithe, it's OK to be befuddled, because we are talking about God here.

How can we possibly understand God and heaven and all that when we've never ever met him or been in the place where he lives?

I don't deliberately set out to upset people, but . . . Actually, that's not true. I do sometimes deliberately set out to upset people, but never to the extent that Jesus did, and only for the best possible reasons. To be honest, that's not true either. On some occasions my motivation has been a bit suspect. Oh, all right, let's start again.

On one of those occasions when I was not deliberately setting out to upset anyone, I managed to rather annoy a man who runs a Christian Healing Centre in North America. I asked him a question about his published account of the amazing things that had been happening there.

'I'm always excited to read about people being helped by God,' I said, 'but I was very struck by the way God himself is described in the book. In terms of personality, I thought he came over as rather bland and characterless. What do you think?'

There are times when it's so inconvenient being a Christian. The poor fellow stiffened visibly, but the spinning cogs of redeemed irritation were not allowed to engage with his face.

'I think most people who've read it think the opposite,' he said with a sacrificial smile and a slight gritting of the teeth. 'After all, it's full of stories about God blessing people. If that's not personality, I don't know what is.'

'Well, that's what I meant, actually. We know – or we hope we know – that God blesses people, but that's not exactly textured, is it? I mean, my mother was very loving to everybody, but so are lots of people. You couldn't have picked my mum out from a crowd with that information, could you?'

The conversation didn't go too well after that. I got the feeling he and I were speaking different languages.

That happens to me quite a lot.

I have had a go at exploring the nature of God in different ways and with varying success (whatever that means), but there is one idea that really appeals to me. I would love to write a book about a junior angel whose first important task is to deliver a copy of *The Times* to God each morning. Weird idea? Yes, but the possibilities are fascinating. The book might be called *Letters from an Angel*, or something equally inspired, and this is how it might begin.

Letters from an Angel

This week, while pursuing my duties as executor of a friend's will, I came across a batch of papers that purport to be letters from some kind of junior angel, writing, from – well, from heaven, I suppose. It would, of course, be absurd to suppose that they are in any sense genuine, but the ones I have had time to read are quite interesting. Perhaps my friend intended them to be published as a book one day. He was a writer. Anyway, here is the most recent of these communications, dealing with an issue that was in the news only a couple of weeks ago. I hope you find it interesting.

Dear George,

Hope you're well. Just thought you'd like to hear about something sort of sad and sweet that happened here in heaven a few weeks ago. By the way, you won't forget your promise, will you? As far as anybody else on earth or heaven is concerned I don't exist. You made me up. And none of the things I write about have really taken place. Thanks. I trust you.

So, this thing that happened. As I've already mentioned to you, my first real job up here is bringing a copy of *The Times* to God every morning to read while he enjoys his Americano with an extra shot. OK, OK, I can see your questions floating up like blue bubbles from the third planet. Does God really drink coffee? Why would he bother to read a newspaper when he knows everything anyway? Are there really mornings in heaven? How can there be if God never sleeps?

I can see how puzzling this all is. My own trips to your world were equally bewildering in the early days. Perhaps it would help if I explain one or two things. First, God is an Earthophile. Always has been. Loves Marmite. Crazy about Fred Astaire and Ginger Rogers. Adores baby kangaroos. Dreams of swimming with dolphins. Fancies himself as a bit of a chef, especially with fish. All those sorts of things. A closet earthling, some might say – but not too loudly. The other thing is that he's capable of enjoying all of those experiences I mentioned if he chooses. He is God, remember. He may know everything and be all-powerful, but if he has a yen to suspend his omnipotence and omniscience while he reads the paper and relaxes, he can do it. Inside that little temporal capsule of coffee-drinking and cross-word-solving he can be as limited and human as he wants. Sleep? Mornings? The essence of all those things can easily be arranged when you're the one who created them in the first place and, as a matter of record, experienced both, every day, for thirty-three years.

Anyway, on this particular morning I happened to glance at the paper just before putting it down on the table next to God. A paragraph on the front page caught my eye. As casually as I could, I tucked the newspaper back under my arm.

'You don't want to read this,' I said, trying to keep the tone of my voice as light as possible. 'There's not a lot in it today. Usual old stuff. Very boring. I'll just go back and drop it off in the angel canteen, shall I?'

'Drop it off in the angel canteen?' he said, raising his eyebrows. 'You know how much I enjoy *The Times* with my coffee.' He tapped the table beside him with one finger. 'Pop it down here, my lad. Don't you dare take my newspaper away.'

I did as I was told. He is God, after all. But I hung about near the door, waiting. Two minutes later the silence was broken.

'Oh, no . . .' His voice was soft with disappointment. 'Oh dear. Such a shame. Such a terrible shame. Makes me feel so sad.'

I really can't stand seeing God unhappy. None of us can. He may be awesome, but he's very nice with it.

'The Girl Guides?' I asked miserably.

He nodded slowly.

'Yes. The thing is, I know they don't always mean it, and lots of them change their minds later on as they get older – they're bound to, aren't they? But I have so appreciated the bit where they promise to love me. I enjoy that. It wafts up before me like a very delicate scent. Fragrant. Soothing. Wonderful. Quite – heavenly, in fact.'

He raised a hand as if to ward off comment.

'And yes, I know all the arguments. Children come from increasingly varied backgrounds. Every religion and none at all. I fully understand the desire to be inclusive. Between you and me, if I was capable of being tempted, I might easily become a Universalist myself. I suppose one of my concerns is that the new Girl Guide promise follows the trend towards an emphasis on self-nurture and development. It says in this article that "I promise to love my God" has become "I promise to be true to myself and develop my talents". Nothing wrong with that in itself, of course, but the thing is that I do actually exist, and I do actually care about them. I have always hoped that those two facts might become part of their lives as they grow up.'

He leaned back and stared at the ceiling.

'Mainly, though, as I said, I shall miss hearing those young, enthusiastic voices promising to love their God. I shall still keep my promise, though. I shall always love them.'

I sensed it was time for me to leave. As I slipped quietly from the room, I couldn't help noticing the large tear that rolled down the face of God, landing with a tiny splash in his untasted Americano.

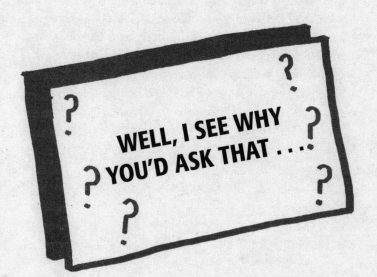

Can I be a Christian if I still have doubts about God existing?

I'm not sure you can be an authentic Christian if you *never* have thoughts that perhaps God doesn't exist, simply because the Christian faith is what it sounds like – faith. That might be an overstatement, because I have met a few souls who say that they never doubt, and I don't question their sincerity or integrity – in fact, I'm really rather envious of them. But for most of us more mortal mortals, I think moments or seasons of doubt are as normal as breathing.

Faith says that one day we will see Jesus, after death, or when he comes again. In the meantime we don't. So experiencing doubt is simply an indication that we don't actually happen to be dead just yet.

Where are all the hot single Christian guys?

Very simple. They got married, got older, and are now in their sixties, busily writing inadequate answers to anguished questions from lonely young Christian people.

Who am I kidding? I was never more than lukewarm, let alone 'hot'. Having said that, there was one famous occasion when my wife Bridget arrived at a crowded meeting and attempted to communicate the fact that I had a high temperature and would be staying at home.

'Adrian's really hot in bed,' she announced brightly.

Her decision to share this apparently gratuitous piece of information must have seemed a little surprising to those present, but I think it might have provoked a round of applause – I can't quite remember.

More seriously, I have known a number of single Christians of all ages who desperately want a special somebody to share their lives, and my heart aches for them. After forty-four years of richly layered marriage I can't even remember how it feels to be single. Our lives have been characterised by mutual support, common interests, occasional cataclysmic rows, and regular re-runs of comfortable old arguments that are more like familiar tunes than serious disagreements. Also, crucially, we have never actually killed each other. This is a frequently under-estimated but essential component of successful marriage.

For single Christians I've spoken to who really do want to 'get it right', there are several recurrent problems. One of these is unhelpful advice from people whose mission in life appears to be doing bodge-up jobs on behalf of a god who can never be seen to fail. Ironic, isn't it, that a feverish and often fear-driven desire to defend some deficient deity can produce such guilt and confusion in those who need support and understanding from a God who is actually as practical and realistic as he is loving?

A common example is the suggestion that 'His grace is sufficient for you'. In other words, being single is OK because we have Jesus. This is a reference to the passage in 2 Corinthians where Paul is describing his thorn in the flesh, and explaining that God has decided not to remove his servant's problem because the weakness, whatever it is (wouldn't we love to know – well, I would!), will make divine power all the more evident. That's what it was about, and it's no use turning up in an exegetical JCB to crudely shovel a random pile of stuff over the top of an issue to which it has no relevance. Jesus was a pragmatist. He may have been God, but he wasn't stupid.

We all need people close to us. Jesus himself did. I certainly do. Very, very few of the people I meet prefer to be on their own. And if you want a clear pointer to the heart of God in this context, it may be worth reflecting on the fact that, in the midst of the mental and physical anguish of the crucifixion, Jesus took a few moments to sort out his mother's domestic arrangements. She needed someone to look after her. Grace in itself was not sufficient, but the practical outworking of grace certainly was.

Grace is like that. It doesn't float around like an abandoned balloon, just being itself. It always does something.

If you are happy on your own, that's fine. But if not, do talk freely to God about the desire of your heart. He will certainly understand, and he might even sort something out.

Another common problem arises from the question of whether or not God chooses a specific partner for each of his followers. I really cannot pretend to know the answer to that question, but I am sure that worrying feverishly about getting it wrong is terribly bad for us. Someone once said that we should pray as though only prayer works, and work as though only work works. I think the same principle might apply to the search for an ideal, divinely selected husband or wife. Keep praying that you won't screw up, and then get on with the business of being with people and enjoy the prospect of meeting somebody wonderful. The ever-ingenious Holy Spirit might write something in the sky for you, but clear guidance seems to be in short supply, other than in the wearyingly popular sense of ascribing divine intervention to random coincidence.

In any case, getting married is a lot like buying a house. You don't really know what it means until you've moved in, and general maintenance can only be learned bit by bit. Human optimism, whether in the world or the Church, can be very comforting. In the event, as most of us discover, the truth is unpredictable and challenging. Marriage can be more costly but also more rewarding than we might have imagined.

And then there's sex. Good old sex. That ever-present,

continually distracting, unbroken-in equine-mount-like activity.

I am reliably informed by young Christian friends of mine that all the stuff about saving yourself for the person you eventually marry is losing its imperative force, even among those who raise their hands and publicly aspire to such a principle. There are, of course, many younger people who are determined that they will not have a sexual relationship before they marry, and I am more than willing to put up with the raucous laughter with which the world will greet my view that they have got their heads screwed on right, and that they should be supported and affirmed in their intentions.

Yes, I know how difficult it is for people of all ages in the present social climate. And yes, I know that there's a lot of hypocrisy in the Church on this subject. And yet another yes – I know that, in the main, we are not talking about folk being evil or predatory. Finally, yes, I am well aware that we who belong to the anxious tribe of Christian Parents have used some pretty spurious arguments in the past in our panic-stricken desire to produce sausage-sizzling, chorus-singing virgins, safe and uncompromised.

In the end there is only one overwhelming reason why Christians should abstain from sex before marriage, and it is quite simply that, as far as we can see, it is what God wants. If you believe that, then don't do it. If you don't believe it – well, do what you like. If you've done it and you wish you hadn't, the good news is that God specialises in new beginnings and is already working on your bespoke, virtual virgin package. He must love it when people start again.

A final point. Some unmarried Christians I know repeatedly take their physical relationship to a screamingly intense pitch, and then stop short of actual intercourse because they don't want to offend God. Well, quite apart from the fact that it must constitute a sort of creeping health hazard, this sort of sweaty madness must be closer to Bill Clinton's definition of 'not having sex' than God's. No one's saying it's easy, but for goodness' sake! Find something equally attractive instead – croissants and hot chocolate, for instance, or a parachute jump, or a perfect cup of tea, or a cold shower. At least you can bring all those things to some sort of conclusion . . .

Yes, all right. I've been married for forty-four years. What do I know? I'll shut up now.

Jeff – does your wife ever tell you that your humour is inappropriate, or has she given up?

One of the most marvellous sights to me is that of my wife, Kay, laughing out loud at a story that she has heard me tell five hundred times. Scratch that. A thousand times. I used to think that she was just giggling dutifully, smiling broadly to be supportive, an act of love and faithfulness, which it is. But she tells me that she still finds the way I put things funny, and she enjoys seeing others enjoying themselves, and so naturally joins in. And I love it when I get to nudge my adult children (and in that I include my wonderful son-in-law Ben, because he is a son and a great friend to me) to laughter, and when my grandchildren giggle at their granddad.

I say all this because then, if I do miss the mark, cross a line or become inappropriate, Kay's gentle words of correction become much easier to respond to, and (note that I've thought very carefully before making this statement) I always listen and respond. That's possible because she mingles unswerving faithfulness with her critique. We've all met people who relish the opportunity to criticise – they are human Tipp-Ex. Even if they do offer encouragement, you know that a 'but' is coming . . .

'I enjoyed what you said today, Jeff, but . . .'

Don't be a 'but' person. Sorry, that came out wrong – you know what I mean.

What's the one thing about you that you'd most like to change?

I rush. I dash. I sprint through my days.

Recently, Her Majesty's government has been trying to help slow me down.

A letter arrived. I stared at the envelope, and tried to halt the rising tide of dread that sickened my stomach.

Printed on the corner of the stern brown stationery was the logo of the Surrey constabulary. Meldrew-like, I could not believe it. I had been caught speeding (again), the hapless victim of a motorway camera.

I won't make light of my crime or try to extract any humour from my being caught. Speeding kills people, and I was guilty, m'lud. Never mind that I was only four miles over the limit, or that it seems like speed cameras have become a major source of income for local authorities these days. That's not the point. I was speeding.

Last time it happened, I was forced to attend a speed awareness course. A sorry, shamed-looking group shuffled into a lecture room for a three-hour event designed to show us just how devastating speed can be. I actually enjoyed the experience, and stayed behind afterwards to thank the instructor for a good evening. He responded by looking at me as if I was quite mad. I graduated from the course (which was no great achievement, because you just have to be there to do so), and vowed that I'd slow down, a pledge that I quickly broke.

I live my life at speed. I eat quickly, and I can't think why. Savouring the flavour of food has never been my style. I wish I could say that I was raised in a large, hungry family, where if you didn't eat your chicken quickly it would be snatched off the plate, but it's just not true. I just race through my food, because I race through everything.

I speed read, preferring to skim over sentences rather than fully digest the words. I multi-task, steam through to-do lists, and fume in rush-hour traffic jams where congestion means that the one thing you can't do is rush. I get things done, only so that I can get on to the next thing. There's always something else to do, somewhere else to go, some other experience that demands that, whatever I'm doing, it won't be for long.

Lately, I've been asking myself: why the haste?

Rushing is an unconscious habit, one that's hard to break. I dash about without thinking. I don't have to be late, under pressure or behind schedule in order to be in a hurry. Slowing down takes a conscious effort. In a world of fast food and high speed Wi-Fi, it's easy to just go with the flow, even – or especially – when the flow is a torrent rather than a trickle.

And then I rush simply because I always have. It's my default setting. I've no idea how long my mother was in labour when I came into the world, but I do know that I arrived early, very prematurely. I strongly suspect I took minutes rather than hours to make my appearance, and having received a slap from the midwife, proceeded to ask when school would be starting.

Then there's the subtle pressure to be busy, because haste offers proof that we are in demand, that those who need us must get in line or take a numbered ticket.

Plus, slowing down is just so hard. When I relax I feel guilty. Going on holiday takes serious mental and emotional preparation. Suddenly finding myself without activity, free of the rush created by rushing, I can spiral down into vague depressiveness, enduring rather than enjoying those lazy days of sunshine.

But as the speed awareness course demonstrated with horrifying illustrations, speed can be truly devastating, and not just on the roads. I've made super-swift decisions that proved to be disastrous, or messes that could have been prevented with a little pause. I've wasted too many beautiful moments because I've not been fully present in them, quickly dashing on to the next thing, which I hoped would be better, but generally was not. Life lived like that becomes something to get through, rather than an experience to savour.

If I want to become more like Jesus, then a better rhythm isn't a luxury. It's a necessity. He knew how to say no; at crucial times he evaded the madding crowds and commanded his friends to come apart for a while, presumably so that they wouldn't fall apart.

So, wish me well as I make my attempt at slowing – life – down.

Right, got to go. Must get on.

Or maybe not.

What prompted you to start writing?

Initially, my marvellous English teacher at school, Mr Ruff. I've tried, unsuccessfully, to track him down, to thank him for his inspirational encouragement.

Adrian nudged me as well. It was so many years ago I'm pretty sure he's forgotten it. Somehow he heard some tapes of me teaching about 'The Father Heart of God', and he contacted me, suggesting that I write. If he ever gets around to reading my bits in this book, he will feel some well-deserved pride – or possibly regret.

I often feel I need to defend God when controversial subjects arise. I don't even know my mind on some things. Any advice?

I am quite a good person to ask about this because I've made such a mess of defending God in the past, mainly by not telling the truth about my own thoughts and feelings, especially when I first became a Christian. In my passionate desire to make this new-found faith of mine appear reasonable and strong and wonderfully shiny to everyone else, I reached out with arguments and declarations that had no real home in my not very agile mind.

It was like being in love. My new beloved could do no wrong, and if I was asked a challenging question to which I had no answer, I would make something up, however facile my argument might be.

Those days are long gone, and although I sometimes envy that foolish young man his blind determination to shore up the entire, unwieldy edifice that is Christianity, the passion does remain, but it is no longer blind. Because of this I deal with parallel realities on a daily basis. One of those realities is a deeply ingrained warmth and affection for the God who has captured my thoughts and energies for the last four decades. The other is an unending and sometimes distressing struggle to understand the best way to speak truthfully about his presence in the world. Where is he? What does he do? What does he not do? Why doesn't he do all the things we believe that we would do if we were as omniscient and omnipotent as he is supposed to be? Why do we so easily descend into neurotically positive drivelling when the truth is too patchy to handle? Why do Christians do so much falling out and arguing about the right way to speak or behave or worship (whatever that means)?

That first reality, the one about relationship with God, is (together with my wife and tea) what sustains me nowadays, even when I stop believing in him for a while. The second one, the mess of questions, is awkward and confusing, but manageable as long as I allow a famous phrase of six words, one that I'm always quoting, to light the way.

The truth will set you free.

Not hectoring, self-righteous truth, but considered truth about everything, positive and negative, that I feel and think about my faith. The truth, however small or ordinary, is invariably almost magically sufficient, and it can affect people very deeply. To the person who originally asked the question I would say this. From your small store give whatever is helpful, but never be afraid to say you don't know, or you don't understand, or that you are seriously conflicted. God is never embarrassed by the truth. Perhaps that is a significant difference between him and us.

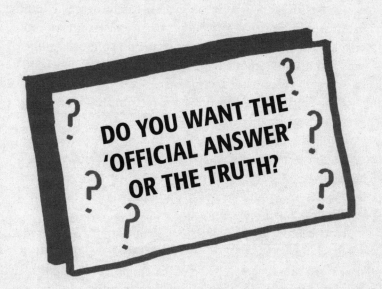

Are you looking forward to dying so that you can be with Jesus?

Absolutely not. Let me make this clear: I do not want to die, and I have no desire to see Jesus today, because the only way to make that encounter happen would be for me to die.

I think that this admission might come as a shock to some, but will certainly bring a sigh of relief for others.

I know that the rules say I ought to follow this statement up by murmuring humbly that I don't want to die because I have much more to do in God's service, which is true, but it's not the whole story. My desire to maintain a pulse is fuelled by more than pious ambition.

I want to live, well, because I want to live: to see my grandsons grow from boys to men, to drink plenty more toasts to setting suns, to have loads more laugh-out-loud moments around log fires with vintage friends. Dying would get in the way of all that. And so, for that matter, would the return of Jesus.

I recently heard of a young lady who felt desperately guilty because she was about to get married and was terrified that Jesus would return before she had had the chance to have sex. Life as we know it would end and the wedding would be cancelled. But her guilt was a burden God didn't want her to carry. He *designed* her to have a longing for her lover. If in doubt, read the Song of Solomon.

As I confess my own lack of enthusiasm about wearing a coffin, I hear someone ask, 'What about Paul and his words, "For me to live is Christ, to die is gain?"'

While I'm filled with admiration for (and somewhat intimidated by) Paul's attitude towards his own demise, his was not some vague death wish. His approach was shaped by a life that at times was filled with gut-wrenching pain, and he struggled with persecution, misunderstandings, false accusations, tensions with close friends, fights that tore churches apart, and personal rejection – some say that he was ostracised and made an outcast by his own family because of his decision to follow Jesus. Life had been terrible for him at times, and he confessed that occasionally he felt so low, it was as if he felt in his heart and mind that he was under a sentence of death. And bear in mind, when he affirmed that death meant gain he was indeed on death row, under house arrest.

Apparently Winston Churchill's last words were, 'I'm so bored of it all.' Perhaps when your life, like Churchill's, like Paul's, is one of unbelievable achievement but starts to feel like a continuous uphill trudge, then you might pine to be out of it all and fully in the presence of Jesus. Perhaps that time will come for me, when my body and mind are terminally tired – and perhaps then I will be more eager to see the face of the One who has changed my life beyond recognition, and will surrender to succumbing with a little more joy. But until that season comes, I desperately, urgently, absolutely want to continue to live that life.

What do you think progress means for Christians?

Good question.

There is an itch that eventually bedevils just about every Christian organisation I have ever been involved with. It starts small, like all the best and worst things in the world. First one person scratches, then another, then three more, and before you can say 'John Robinson' the whole assembly is playing a frenetic game of spiritual Twister.

It happened during that period in the 1980s and '90s when everyone in the more intentionally spontaneous churches seemed to be talking about the 'Toronto Blessing', a wave of the Spirit that originated in the Airport Church of Toronto in Canada. So anxious were some congregations in the United Kingdom to obtain and own this phenomenon that they actually dispatched one or more of their ministers or elders to North America to, as it were, get it and bring it back.

Puzzling, isn't it? One can only suppose that the Holy Spirit was unable to obtain the appropriate export licence. Or possibly God, taking his lead from one or two American Christian publishers, was unwilling to waste his time and resources on a market that was too small and unprofitable to make it worth his while. Who knows?

This ecclesiastical impetigo is about change and progress and moving forward and expanding and achieving success, whatever that might mean, and it happens in churches of every size and variety. It looks like such a good idea, and as long as all those thrusting, breathless things are servants rather than masters, I welcome them. I myself would be unable to build a sandpit in a desert, but I do recognise that things need to be done properly.

No, the problem comes when human ambition and optimism overtake spiritual common sense and a clear vision of what it means to be Jesus for the people we encounter and serve as his representatives.

At Scargill House, the North Yorkshire holiday and conference centre that Bridget and I have been closely involved with for the last five years, there are regular discussions about the direction and aims of the institution. Where is it best to place and use our effort and resources? Which aspects of our ministry need to be changed or tweaked so that fundamental aims will continue to be achieved? Is there scope for expansion and outreach to other parts of the area in which we live?

These are all good questions to ask and, if possible, to answer, but I suggest that all Christian organisations should begin with a clear and uncluttered understanding of what 'success' and 'reaching our goals' means in the kingdom of God.

The fact is that if Scargill closed tomorrow, five years after reopening in 2010, it would nonetheless have been successful for each visitor or guest who has been touched by God, in whatever way it happened. In that sense, through the grace of God, we reach our goal almost every day.

We know that because our example is Jesus. After those three years of intensive ministry many may have thought and some undoubtedly said that the whole thing had ended in disaster. And in the world's eyes, they were right. A promising career was abruptly curtailed, firstly by ignominious death and secondly by total disintegration of morale among those who had followed Jesus only for as long as the going was safe and good.

There were many, however, who would not have agreed with that view. The lepers who were healed, the woman rescued from stoning after being accused of adultery, the widow of Nain whose son was raised from the dead and given back to her, the guests at the Cana wedding who saw a conjuring trick to beat all conjuring tricks, the Syro-Phoenician woman who begged Jesus for her daughter's life and was granted her wish – all of these and countless others recorded and unrecorded, whether they followed future events or not, would have said that, far from being a disaster, the ministry of Jesus changed their lives for ever.

How were they to know that the ultimate goal for Jesus, to die and to be raised to life, would make it possible for these miracles to continue over the next two thousand years all over the world, and to still be happening at places like Scargill House in 2015?

We find it very difficult to absorb and comprehend the staggering, topsy-turvy, upside-down, paradoxical truth that the vast, cosmically significant fact of the death and resurrection of Jesus Christ occurred precisely so that, through his followers, he could continue to walk the streets of every country in the world, having small encounters with broken people and introducing the power of fresh hope into their lives.

Two thousand years ago a poor, elderly woman put two coins into the temple offering. It was all she had. Jesus told his disciples that she had given more than any of the rich people who were ostentatiously donating a tiny fraction of their total wealth. When Jesus said that she had given more than any of the others he was not speaking comparatively. That was not his way. He was saying that the benefit of that gift would be greater than anyone could have imagined. And of course, he was right. That woman has been seated in heaven for twenty decades listening to people discussing, describing and learning lessons from that one small sacrificial act. A cosmic consequence from a mustard seed of giving.

Jesus did not die so that church leaders could create empires. He did not go through Gethsemane so that epic plans and immense organisational feats could take the place of chats with the person next to you on the bus. He did not give up the warmth of human companionship and the love of a good woman in order that something tidy, programmed and loveless could grow so efficiently that it loses touch with its roots and forgets why it was there in the first place.

Be careful with that itch. It could be catching.

I should add that when I was less than ten years old I received an unsigned gift from God. Put simply, it was the shocking awareness that every single person in the world is the star, the leading player, in his or her own little world. Jesus died so that we could understand how important each of these little worlds is to him. Our task is to recognise their value in his eyes. We are to enter these worlds and make sure God's stars understand just how deeply they are loved. If we do that we have come close to understanding and discovering the secret of success.

We can certainly help to build God's kingdom, but unless we accept that he is the architect we are wasting our time. Grasping this essential truth is a clear sign of progress.

Have you ever faked a Holy Spirit manifestation?

Without a doubt. During the early 1990s, when the so-called 'Toronto Blessing' was in full swing, I was swinging, as it were, in the middle of it. Those were exciting days, with such an amazing, tangible sense of the presence of God around. I was privileged to speak at a number of conferences at the then Toronto Vineyard Church, the place where the strange manifestations began. At first, it all seemed very authentic. There were a few daft things going on too, and critics of the movement made much of the occasional aberration, but it was also a time when many people experienced a tangible touch from God.

I remember the first time that Kay and I met Carol and John Arnott, the pastors at Toronto. They were speaking at a conference that I was also addressing in Ireland. At the end of one of the evenings, I was eager for some end-of-the-day luxury, like some fine cheese and a pleasant glass of Merlot, but John and Carol asked if we would like them to pray for us. Suspending my pursuit of a late-night snack for a while, we readily agreed. What followed was an experience of about thirty minutes of raw power pulsing through our bodies, as Kay and I were filled with waves of the Holy Spirit. It was unforgettable, not just because of the experience, but because of the fruit that followed: the effect on Kay was most dramatic – from that day, exhibiting a greater sense of confidence in life, ministry and marriage (I no longer get away with what I used to, which I am mostly glad about).

But there were elements of the movement that became unhealthy, at least in my view. When tens of thousands of people gather from all across the world on the hunt for God, inevitably there will be some who are fanatical, unbalanced or emotionally unhealthy. Such extremes inevitably fuelled the fire built by the critics.

Certainly at times there was public pressure to 'have an experience'. Sometimes, before preaching, I would be prayed for by whoever was leading the service. With thousands of people looking on and the television cameras running, there is quite a pressure to have *something* happen, whether or not it is genuine, especially when it is guaranteed that some will judge you negatively if you're prayed for and nothing ensues. It's difficult to speak with credibility to a conference full of people who insist that they are in the centre of the proverbial river of the Spirit, if they are thinking that you are high and dry on the far bank. I honestly don't think that I put on a show or performed to order when prayed for on those public platforms, but I can't be sure that mine was not an unconsciously Pavlovian response. 'Pavlovian' as in the psychologist with his obedient dogs. Not as in crispy white meringues.

But there were times when I was just in line for prayer with everyone else, when I did take what I might call a 'courtesy drop' and just took a backwards dive, having checked, of course, that a catcher was dutifully standing by. There was a lot of emphasis on 'falling under the power' or 'being slain in the Spirit' (a term I hate, because it sounds a little like Ananias and Sapphira dropping dead as a result of their financial conniving). Whatever the preacher talked about, be it marriage, justice, prayer or whatever, people would line up at the end so that the ministry team could do their thing – and everyone would end up on the carpet.

Some of those ministry team people were tenacious souls, as eager for a result as a group of tenpin bowlers keen to see the pins topple on a Friday night. They'd pray, shout, blow on you, whisper in your ear: frankly they wouldn't leave you alone until you hit the deck. Like a rash that won't succumb to cream, they were not going anywhere until you crumpled to the floor. And those meetings could go late into the night, and I had cheese and wine waiting.

So, there were a few times when I took a dive.

Don't judge me too harshly. I got a nap. The ministry team member got a result. Win win.

And, half an hour or so later, back in the hotel room, the Stilton was delicious.

Will only Christians go to heaven?

I am not in charge of this decision, for which I thank God. However, you won't be surprised to hear that I have a view. I always have a view. Like most of my views, this one seems to flicker as I attempt to adjust the focus, but I offer it to you for what it may be worth.

Many Christians seem to find themselves drifting into a gentle haze of Universalism as they become older. Generally speaking, they don't actually claim that every-one in the universe will be saved, but there is a sense that lines are redrawn, certainties diluted and old questions reopened. One of these benevolently liberal believers, a man who died many years ago, attracted much of the loving venom that only Christians can produce when they are too insecure to explore their own instincts. Seated in a corner of our local pub once, I asked him why, in his advanced years, he continued to air views that attracted such acrimony. As far as I can recall through a miasma of fading memory and beer fumes, the conversation proceeded as follows.

'Well,' he said, in the deliberately gentle, non-combative tones that so often annoyed his critics, 'I suppose someone needs to speak up for God now and then.'

'But that's why they get cross with you, isn't it? They say you're not speaking up for God at all. You're watering down the gospel. Jesus is the only way to salvation. Anyone who doesn't ask him into their lives is lost. Are they wrong?'

He stared into the remainder of his pint of Harvey's for a moment, apparently hypnotised by its golden promise. Finally he spoke.

'Adrian, I think it began when I noticed that verse in Peter's first letter, saying God is not willing that any should be lost. I let those words roll around my head for a while, and then I tried to look honestly at how they made me feel. Mostly, I felt sorry for God. I really did. The omnipotent, omniscient God wants everyone to be saved, everyone from Genghis Khan to Patience Strong. Don't look so sceptical – surely even Patience Strong must have had a soul? Anyway, that's what he wants, and that's why he became a man who died and came back to life. The logic of that defeats me as much as it should any honest person, but the fact remains that he did it to give his dream a chance of being fulfilled. I hate the thought of him being disappointed. Don't you?'

'Well yes, but are you saying all mankind will be saved regardless of whether they become Christians or not? I mean, that verse only says God doesn't want anyone to be lost. It doesn't say that he intends to make that happen, does it?'

'No, it doesn't. Clearly omnipotence has its limits. No, I suppose I just wanted to help God by flagging up his motivation in all this. We Christians happily parrot those words about God loving the world so much that he gave his only beloved Son, but we may have lost sight, if we ever had it, of the epic passion behind those iconic verses. I like to remind certain people that the God they claim to serve is probably greater and more passionately welcoming than their narrow-eyed scrutiny of the spiritual rules and regulations might suggest. The whole idea, believe it or not, is to bring us home, not to study our papers and decide we can't come in because our handwriting has crept over the edge of one small box relating to prejudice against waterfowl.'

'Stop making me laugh and answer my question. Before I get another round in, tell me if Jesus is the only way to home or heaven or whatever you call it.'

My friend leaned back and gazed into the distance. When he spoke at last there was a sweet sadness in his tone.

'Oh, you are such a very cruel man, Adrian,' he said with a smile, 'but OK – after all, a pint of Harvey's is marginally more alluring than the Holy Grail.'

He continued with meticulous deliberation.

'The older I get, the more I am sure, in my heart of heart of hearts, that Jesus is indeed the only means by which we wretched, beloved humans will eventually be able to breathe an eternal sigh of relief. There! Good news for those who want to tidy my theology.

'The bad news – news that will have those same people scratching their heads and frowning through a concordance, and checking with the elders, and praying for my eternal soul – is this. The older I get, the more I am equally sure that I have no idea what being saved by Jesus might mean. I have this blasphemous idea in my head, you see, that God might do exactly what he wants in exactly the way he chooses. C.S. Lewis talked about expecting surprises in heaven. An understatement, surely. When God casts a net on the right side of his boat the size and variety of the catch will be astonishing. Many will disagree with me, and they may be right. If I turn out to be in error I shall discuss the matter with my heavenly Father over a pint of real ale in due course.

'So, you must admit that I have at least tried to answer two difficult questions. Your round, I think.'

They do flicker slightly, don't they, the things my friend said? But I value the spirit of his wisdom, if you know what I mean. It may feel unsafe to throw open the windows and allow fresh air in when we are busy creating a world where Christianity can only be safely enjoyed at room temperature, but that kind of caution can have a stifling effect. Besides, as far as this question is concerned, it's worth bearing in mind that we are the ones who create and put on these spiritual identification labels we set so much store by. God is the one who will eventually take them off.

Do you speak in tongues?

Yes I do, and I find it very helpful, not least because otherwise I often don't pray, just because I can't think of anything intelligent to say, or life has rendered me somewhat speechless. And I find speaking in tongues to be a vital experience when I am desperate, or urgently need God's help.

But let me be totally honest and take a risk with you. I've never got around to saying this before, either in public speaking or in print, but here goes: I'm not totally sure that the 'prayer language' I use really comes from God.

Speaking in tongues sometimes seems like a totally absurd thing to do, and perhaps it's OK to say that, because mouthing syllables and believing that somehow they come as a result of the Holy Spirit's activity is an act of faith, and just as faith itself occasionally feels quite ridiculous and daft, so does the practice of speaking in tongues.

There are occasions when I just think I'm speaking gobbledegook in an affected Middle Eastern accent. This is not helped by the way that I began speaking in tongues, just after becoming a Christian. In those days, seeking to be 'baptised in the Spirit' usually meant either going forward at the end of a service to be prayed for by a person who would encourage you to speak out whatever strange words formed in your mind, or going to what used to be called a 'tarrying meeting' where a group of people, eager for the power and 'the gift', would gather. There would be a time of encouragement, teaching and then prayer. Muttering one or two odd words would usually lead to congratulations: 'You've got it now.' Any doubts that we were just making the words up would be silenced by using the Scripture, 'Which of you, if your son asks for bread, will give him a stone? . . . How much more will your Father in heaven give good gifts to those who ask him!' (Matthew 7:9, 11)

The logic went like this:

1. You've asked God to fill you with his Spirit.
2. He is keen to do that.

3. *Something* has happened.
4. You must not call what has happened anything other than the work of the Spirit, because that would be questioning God's ability and willingness to give. You've asked for a loaf of Hovis; he wouldn't give you a brick.

But here's my niggling question: why was receiving this gift supposed to be so very easy, when so many other things that we beg God for – direction, rescuing trafficked children, healing for my friend Anthony, who is battling cancer – are not so easily come by? If the supernatural is on tap that readily, why don't we see more answers in other areas where it is so desperately needed?

Lest anyone is tempted to ring round and organise a modern-day stoning, let me affirm that I totally believe that the power and gifts of the Holy Spirit are available for us today. It's just that I wonder if they are as readily available from God's vending machine as we often suggest. When God wants to speak, he'll speak – he'll choose the how and when.

But here's the further confession that might make some want to pick up a pebble and lob it in my direction: while I'm not sure if my experience of speaking in tongues is necessarily a Holy Spirit gift, I'm not totally sure that it matters.

God knows my heart. He knows that I want to cry out to him, to worship him, to urgently request his help. So even if I am just mouthing syllables that I've subconsciously made up, or even copying what I've heard others say when they've prayed, would it really matter?

What does count is the recognition that I need to be filled with the Holy Spirit, genuinely and authentically, each and every day of my life.

Adrian, we are a new church. How can we make sure that, in our ministry to others, the policies we adopt properly represent the will of God?

One of the features that seems to be absent in far too much of what we call Christian ministry is the simple belief that there really is a God, who really is present when we talk or pray or eat or play badminton or chop vegetables or sing Handel's *Messiah* with people. It seems reasonable to assume that this God has a specific view of each situation, and a specific notion of what might be the best approach to take with the person or people concerned.

When this fundamental assumption is lacking, we become hungry for policies. We want to know what to think and what to say, how to react and how to proceed. The theory is that once we have our checklist we can simply apply it to any issue or problem that is presented to us. That is why, in the context of our normal expectations, God appears to be randomly and sometimes disturbingly disruptive.

It was ever thus. In the ninth chapter of John's Gospel, Jesus and the disciples come across a man blind from birth. A loose paraphrase of the question asked by the disciples and the reply they get from Jesus might be as follows.

'Ah, a man blind from birth. So what's the policy here, then, Lord? Somebody's fault, obviously, so would that be the man himself, or his parents?'

'Neither,' says Jesus, perhaps a little wearily, 'but his blindness is a chance for the world to see the good things of God.'

The man is healed, and his subsequent encounter with the infuriated Pharisees is one of the few truly funny passages in the New Testament. Real pantomime stuff. Read it. Imagine it.

Even more instructively for those of us who truly want to understand and try to represent the heart of God, in the previous chapter we hear about an adulterous woman who has been dragged along by the Pharisees so that Jesus can be trapped into speaking out against the Law. Those guys must have felt very confident about their ploy. They believed they knew three things for sure, and they were absolutely right.

The first was that the punishment for adultery was stoning. Correct. The Law of Moses was quite clear.

The second was that Jesus had revealed himself to be a man who, because of his compassion towards wrongdoers and his profound abhorrence of cruelty, would never be able to sit quietly by and allow a woman to be stoned to death in front of his eyes.

Thirdly, he had carefully made clear that his teaching was not in conflict with the Law. On the contrary, he publicly declared that it was easier for heaven and earth to disappear than for the least stroke of a pen to drop out of the Law.

So, there it was. They'd got him. If he tried to save her he would be identified as one who sided with law-breakers. If he agreed with the stoning he would deny his own nature and the force of his teaching would be significantly diluted. Allow me a little more paraphrasing. The internal grammar of what happened seems to have gone like this.

'We were just wanting to check with you,' say the Pharisees innocently, 'about the correct policy with this woman who has committed adultery. Er, stoning, isn't it – according to the Law, that is?'

Jesus doodles distractedly in the dust a bit, and says nothing. Slightly uneasy clearing of throats all round.

'So, should we start the stoning, or . . .'

Jesus looks up.

'Sorry? Oh, the stoning. Well, yes. As you say, that's the Law. Better get on with it. So, who's going to start? Oh, I know. What about this? Whichever one of you has never committed a sin – you can be the first one to throw a stone. OK? Sorted! I'll just get back to my writing.'

You know the ending. There is no stoning. The woman goes off to sort out her life. The policy concerning adultery as stated in the Law remains intact, but the higher, heavenly policy of love and redemption has worked its magic.

And, just to add a little more glorious confusion to the whole thing, there are times when that example of love and redemption is somewhat more difficult to follow.

'Master, these money-changers and dove-salesmen here in the temple courtyard – would you like us to invite them to spend some time with us in an encounter group so that we can feed them with fish and lovingly explain that their behaviour falls a tad short of the spiritual ideal?'

'Actually, my idea was to get a knotted rope and beat them out of the place after tipping their tables over and kicking their filthy money around a bit. I will not have my Father's place or my Father's people treated like this, and that's that. I might tell them I love them afterwards . . .'

The lessons for us from all this seem pretty clear to me.

First, we are not called upon to police the lives of those who come to us for help. If he does not condemn, then how in the blue blazes (as my mother used to say) can we? I have known many Christians – and been one myself in the past – who are so nervous of letting God down by appearing to condone sin that they allow no room for the sympathetic, ingenious, transforming power of the Holy Spirit. Bit of a waste, isn't it?

Having said that, there will be occasions when some very straight talking is required. Bridget and I have experienced this on a few occasions. Our priority at those times is to check continually that the agenda we are following is not our own.

The bottom line – and this is bad news for those who love neat solutions and clear boundaries – is that no easily identifiable bottom line is to be found. There is no way of knowing what God will do in any given situation, whatever he may have done last Thursday or the Tuesday before that. Issues of adultery will not be solved by applying the 'Drawing in the dust, not saying anything, then saying something, and then drawing in the dust again' method. It won't work. Something else will work. Nor is it any use throwing tables around when people misuse their power. The appropriate response will be different. The solution will be tailored to the situation. Annoying, isn't it? But quite exciting as well.

So, what might this mean in practice? Good question. I've been trying to think of a relevant example. I do recall a moment in Northern Ireland when I was sitting with two quite elderly men called Brian and William who had come to ask for prayer, but were reluctant to express their problem unless I was able to promise that our conversation would remain confidential. I always explain to people in this situation that, unless it is a problem for them, Bridget and I tell each other everything. Very few people seem to mind. These two fellows certainly didn't. Even so, the silence before either of them spoke was lengthy. Silences can be very fragile. Breaking them is not usually a helpful thing to do.

'The thing is,' said Brian at last, 'William and I are, you know – well, we're one of those what they call same-sex couples. Have been for years and years. Folk in our church think we're cousins because . . . well, because . . .'

'Because that's what we've told them,' said William quietly. 'If they knew the truth there'd be no place for us in the church here, not unless we . . . changed. They're very hot on that sort of thing. We've been here all our lives.'

'Anyway,' continued Brian, his voice breaking very slightly, 'William here has had some tests. And it's bad news. Cancer. We . . . he might have six months. We wanted someone to know all about us, and suggest what we should do, and . . . just say a little prayer . . .'

In the course of answering another question in this book I was trying to describe how reluctant I am to state definitively that God has spoken to me. Using my trade-mark get-out clause, I would say that if God does speak to cloth-eared Christians like me, and if he spoke on this occasion, this is what he said:

'Leave them alone. Just – leave them alone. I love these two fellows and I don't want any great truth-telling sessions or sledgehammer ministry ruining the last part of their lives together. Say a prayer, wish them well, and give them my love. The rest is nothing to do with you.'

My imagination? Could be. Paul says that faith, hope and love are the only things that last. Not much about certainty. I always retreat from certainty. It's a policy with me.

What is the benefit in fasting?

Absolutely none that I can think of, and personally I'm against it. I rather fear that there's been a terrible spelling error, resulting in thousands depriving themselves of food for centuries, and all because of a 'Friday afternoon' scribal error. It should read *feasting,* not *fasting*.

Actually, despite my flippant comments about not approving of the practice, Jesus does approve of it, which rather obviously is far more important. He assumed that those who follow him would fast, as the Sermon on the Mount illustrates. He doesn't say 'if' you fast, but 'when'.

Oh dear. He was, and is, counting on those who follow him to step away from the trough for a while. So, why?

Well, on the few occasions when I have fasted (note that I could have worded this sentence differently, and frankly was tempted to do so, to give the impression that I was a reluctant but regular faster) I *have* found focus and clarity as a result. Fasting is for us, not for God. It's not spiritual blackmail, an intercessory hunger strike calculated to turn God's head and twist his arm. Interrupting the incessant journey of fork to mouth and back to plate is a useful discipline. Food can control us, and so fasting enables us to see who, or what, is in charge of our lives.

In this discipline, though, I have failed miserably, and can only aim to do better.

I'm embarrassed as I remember a time when, as a very young pastor, I and some other ministry colleagues decided that we would pray and fast until we saw spiritual breakthrough in our city. There was nothing casual about our strategy. The married ones among us told our wives that we were going to hole up in the flat of one of the single pastors, and we would not return home until we felt our work was done, no matter how many days or weeks it would take.

Of course there were two significant problems with this unbridled enthusiasm. Firstly, we had only had a little experience with extended times of fasting before (and by 'extended' I mean missing the odd meal and occasionally not eating for a day). And then there was the other challenge that none of us had reckoned with. We had no idea what the 'spiritual breakthrough' that we were so earnestly seeking might look like, so we'd really have no clue about when to actually quit.

We bade farewell to our wives, tearfully saying that we were not sure how long it would be before we saw them again. Their knowing smiles suggested that they knew it wouldn't be too long at all. The fact that we didn't take a change of clothes or our toothbrushes suggested that we knew our extended prayer time would last for a matter of hours rather than turning into weeks of fervent wrestling in prayer.

And our wives were quite right. We prayed for a few hours, oh, quite late into the evening. After a while, we felt the lack of words, and our rumbling stomachs felt a lack of food. When you're very deliberately choosing not to eat, your appetite is heightened. You know that you're hungry when you start looking at the couch as a potential snack.

And then the releasing moment came. One of us spoke up, at first with hesitation, looking around the room for endorsement, not wanting to be the one to break up the foodless party too quickly. But the group agreed with the tentative announcement, as one among us spoke: 'Guys, I just sense that our work is done here. Our prayers have been heard. Let's go home and get some sleep . . .' (Note the unspoken addition to the sentence, '. . . and eat.')

And thus we were soon reunited with our still grinning and completely unsurprised wives, grateful to the one who had shared the 'prophetic' insight that meant we could end our brief monastic time.

You may be wondering who spoke up that night. And I'm terribly embarrassed to say – it was me.

What is your favourite film?

I so wanted to come up with something that made me sound like a sophisticated cinematic connoisseur. An obscure French movie from the 1960s would have been perfect, preferably one that had no identifiable storyline or meaning. Mind you, that could probably have been *any* French film from the 1960s. Or perhaps something obviously positive and heartwarming, like *The Shawshank Redemption*. An older movie, like *Casablanca*. I really didn't get into *Lord of the Rings* (I got bored of the rings, boom boom), I enjoyed *Back to the Future*, and I quite liked *Forrest Gump*, although it did go on for ever. *The Sound of Music* was and is beautiful. I sat through *It's a Wonderful Life* and found it less than wonderful.

On the darker side, *The Silence of the Lambs* and *A Clockwork Orange* chilled me; the latter prompted real fear about the future. I still shudder when I see a chap wearing a bowler hat.

So my favourite film, the one that I've watched dozens of times? In our family and friendship circle, we quote lines from it endlessly. I even have some of the original pages of the studio promotional pack, complete with still slides and black-and-white photos from the set, mounted and framed in my home. It's called *So I Married an Axe Murderer*, which is not the horror flick that its title suggests, but a witty, clever send-up of San Francisco artsy pomposity.

This flick, starring Mike Myers and Nancy Travis, is my all-time favourite, mainly because, as one critic (who thought the film was a 'trifle' but enjoyed it nevertheless) remarked, the gifted actors all just seem to be having such a jolly good time. Does it have a deep, profound message? Not at all. Is the directing, writing or acting worthy of an Oscar? No. And the film was actually a commercial flop, costing twenty million dollars to make, but only grossing eleven million dollars in the US.

But it makes me laugh, no matter how many times I see it. Not everything has to be purposeful, meaningful or significant.

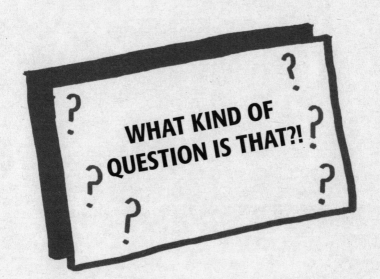

WHAT KIND OF
QUESTION IS THAT?!

Jeff, do you wear eyeliner when preaching?

I know it might be difficult to believe that this is a real question, but it really did come in during one of the *Seriously Funny* evenings. I kept the card to prove it.

No, I don't use eyeliner. But lipstick is another matter . . .

Seriously, the answer is a rather obvious *no*. If I was wearing make-up, the result would not be the facial arrangement that is mine.

Even if I had the money, I wouldn't choose to have 'work' done – despite my sporting a nose that can see around corners and could have been the inspiration for the design of a couple of particularly tricky ski-runs I know of. Too many growing-old-gracefully icons have been turned into permanently grinning – or, in the odd case, mildly terrified-looking – souls by the plastic surgeon's knife.

Are you a bigger person in real life than you are on screen?

I'm unsure whether this refers to personality or sheer physical size. If the former, I suppose I would have to say that I can be disappointingly two-dimensional on occasions, usually when people who have read my books are standing around waiting for me to be funny or profound. The worst of this experience is when I say something banal to fill the echoing silence, and people laugh loudly or nod appreciatively, as though in sympathy. What they say when they get home I dread to think.

'He must get someone else to write his books. He's about as funny as a pencil, or possibly a bus.'

Never mind. The Danish philosopher and theologian Søren Kierkegaard said that no writer is able to equal the content of his own books. Too right, Søren. You and I would have had a great time down the pub with a couple of pints and a bowl of nuts.

If the question is about physique, you can mind your own business – in love.

Which Bible stories make you smile?

There are some tragi-comic moments in the Bible, but you need to have a rather dark sense of humour to appreciate them. The chap who popped into what he thought was a refreshment tent and got a tent-peg through the head probably brings a guilty, wry smile for those who like Hitchcock. Then there's the hapless sword-swinging of Peter as he lashed out to defend his friend Jesus, resulting in the neat amputation of a chap's ear, who probably hollered at volume. I love to read about the healing of that ear, imagining Jesus sticking it back on the side of his head, and the look of astonishment that the briefly one-eared gentleman must have had at that point. He who has ears to hear, let him hear. Now that fellow had a full set again.

But my favourite story isn't dark, and it's not exactly laugh-out-loud funny either. The story of Zacchaeus always brings a smile to my face. It's that episode, much beloved by Sunday school teachers everywhere, where crooked taxman Zacchaeus clambered up a tree to see Jesus, and then did a climb-down – in more ways than one – when Jesus invited himself over for lunch. It was a life-changing meal, leading to the diminutive little swindler nearly emptying his bank account. When the real Jesus stops by your place, your world might just stop, and then get realigned on a new axis.

When I think of that man parked up in the branches, hoping for a better view, I think of Danny DeVito up in a tree. But what really causes me to smile – perhaps a smile birthed from relief rather than humour – is the way that the crooked taxman acted towards Jesus. Rob Parsons has said that it's not so much a miracle that Jesus wanted to be around sinners, but more incredible that rampant, hard-faced sinners wanted to be around Jesus. They felt so very much at home with him. It was the religious crowd who shuffled uncomfortably in his presence, rolled their eyes and released a volley of pious tut-tuts.

Sometimes the Jesus in my mind, the one my imagination conjures up, isn't a chap you'd want to have a meal with.

He becomes the interrogator, even the wide-eyed inquisitor, firing hostile questions.

The employer barking endless orders, hands on hips, nostrils flared, scouring through charts and studying reports, never satisfied by what he sees.

The sour judge, a look of disgust permanently etched in his face, ominously eager to don the black cap and announce the death penalty.

But Zacchaeus experienced a different Jesus. One to relax with.

'More wine, Lord? How do you like those olives? Perhaps some pitta bread? How about if I give most of my ill-gotten gains away? Sorry, I didn't get anything for dessert. I hadn't planned on inviting guests over. Actually, Jesus, I hadn't thought that anyone, let alone you, would *invite himself* over.'

I like the wry smile that comes from dwelling on some of the more macabre Bible stories.

But the smile of relief that comes from pondering the real, beautiful Jesus is better.

Are you a fan of science fiction and fantasy?

So nice to be asked a question that doesn't arrow straight in on God. He must be relieved as well.

I was about to answer a firm 'no' to both parts of the question. I tend to regard most of the modern science fiction I encounter as little more than Tolkien on speed. However, as is becoming apparent with so many of these questions, the correct answer is a little more elusive than that.

When I was much younger I enjoyed the nerve-racking feasibility of Isaac Asimov's work, and was positively mesmerised by Ray Bradbury's darkly whimsical short stories. In my early teenage years the very first book I bought as a result of reading a review in a newspaper was Bradbury's collection of tales entitled *The October Country*. I particularly recall shivering deliciously over a story called 'The Crowd', about a man who notices some-thing odd about the people who collect around motor accidents. Read the story if you think you can handle knowing what that odd thing was.

I found these beautifully written excursions into the far reaches of imagination very inspiring. How exciting to know that the boundaries of experience and perceived reality could be extended and reshaped simply by the writer's decree that it should be so. Why would you not want to do that for the rest of your life?

I had already known the exhilaration of such possibilities at a much younger age when I came across Lewis Carroll's two great classics of fantasy, *Alice's Adventures in Wonderland* and *Through the Looking Glass*. In the first of these Alice is dozing on the river bank when she sees a white rabbit dressed in human clothes hurrying away to an urgent appointment. When he disappears down a rabbit hole Alice follows, and finds herself falling into a hall in a strange world where she is surrounded by doors of many sizes. Through one of these, an opening much too small for her to pass through, she sees a beautiful garden. After drinking from a bottle marked DRINK ME, she begins to shrink at an alarming rate and is only able to halt and reverse the process by consuming a cake that bears the legend EAT ME.

By the time I reached this early point in the story I was hooked for ever. I suppose it was the literary equivalent of a modern computer game. Reality was not in charge of developments. Anything could happen, and so much did, culminating with Alice's triumphant cry of realisation, 'You're nothing but a pack of cards!' I can still recall the mixture of relief and disappointment when I first read these words, relief because the nightmare-tinged fantasy was safely packed away inside the covers of a book, and disappointment for exactly the same reason.

After reading both of the *Alice* books three or four times each, I felt cold and lost. No more Alice! Lewis

Carroll was beyond the reach of readers and publishers. Nothing more to be hoped for from him.

There had to be more Alice! But how?

Rather ambitiously, I started work on *Alice in Riverland*, the story of a little girl who, after falling fast asleep in a rowing boat, topples over the side and discovers a strange, dream-like world at the bottom of the river.

This unfinished masterpiece has, perhaps thankfully, not survived the years, but the spark that ignited it remains like a pilot light in what I am pleased to call my creative consciousness. Looking back, I realise that something quite fundamental had happened inside my small but yearning soul. Fiction, and fantasy fiction in particular, had gifted me with an unexpected pathway to freedom. If and when I ever became a real writer, I would be in charge. I would call the shots.

Mind you, God turned out to have something to say about that.

Where did you have your first kiss and from whom?

It was from a rather lovely girl at a cowboy party at the comprehensive school I attended. I won't name her, because someone from my schooldays might read this and recognise the name. I think I was sixteen, and was dressed in Western wear, including a red scarf around my neck and a hat that could have eclipsed the sun. It was quite a miracle that I got kissed by anybody or anything, considering how ridiculous I looked. And the rim of the huge hat could have knocked somebody unconscious if they got within hand-shaking, never mind kissing, range. If memory serves me right, it was a rather delicious kiss, but regretfully, I acted like quite the cad afterwards. I think the aforementioned young lady thought that our rather brief lip-locking meant that there was a relationship between us, but I (because my friends were giving me a rough time about the furtive snog) chose to completely ignore her the next day. A few years after leaving school, I saw her in the street, and she fixed her eyes on mine, obviously recognising me as the bounder who kissed and ran. She stared me down, and then completely ignored me. And I don't blame her a bit.

How do you sound so spontaneous every night?

How does a large ham manage to glisten so seductively when it is covered in honey glaze and placed in a hot oven? Does that answer your question?

When and where do you feel most close to God?

That's an awkward question. I'm never terribly confident about the authenticity of my feelings. Sometimes, I think I sense God's closeness, and the hint of his voice, but then again, I can't be quite sure whether those feelings are generated from what we broadly describe as the presence of God, or if the source of what I feel comes from elsewhere; my circumstances being stable for a little while, the distant outrageous splash of a riotous sunset, the cosy warmth that comes from a crackling log fire and a shared glass of fine wine with friends, or the key change during the worship set. (Sometimes, during worship, when we go up from C to D, I cry. That's just the way it is.) And knowing Adrian's profound affection for a decent cup of tea – an affection that I share – I should add that to the mix too.

Two key questions arise:

(a) Am I just projecting God into the pleasant sense of well-being that comes when one or more of the above good things happens?

(b) Or did God arrange sunsets/fine wine/tea/musical key changes as a way of helping us to feel closer to him?

Speaking of Adrian, years ago he told me that my feelings were not the barometer of my spirituality, which was certainly a liberating conversation.

So I love the warm fuzzies, but I don't completely trust them.

That said, there are times when I definitely sense God close. I'd like to say that this happens when I'm on an extended monastic retreat on a lonely Gaelic-speaking island way north of anywhere, but this would be a lie, as I've never been on a monastic retreat in any location, mainly because those monkish cells are just too quiet and don't come with TV, let alone Sky.

There is one place where I do tend to feel God close, but it's not a geographical location. Sharing it feels risky, but here goes.

I feel closest to God when I have failed.

When I've messed up, intentionally or unwittingly, when I've said or done the wrong thing, when I feel smeared with shame because of a poor choice, when I feel most dismal and disqualified from being a part of the family of God – that's when I feel him close.

That's scary to say, because it might suggest that we should sin our brains out in order to feel God near, and of course that's not the idea at all. Scripture warns us against thoughtless hedonism: 'Shall we go on sinning, so that grace may increase?'[1]

But stop right there. Is it possible that this warning had to be given precisely because a sense of grace really does multiply when we know we've messed up? When did the prodigal feel closest to his father, most grateful, most

---

1   Romans 6:1

relieved? It was after that turgid excursion via the pig pen. In contrast, his self-righteous elder brother found himself outside the party, stranded by his own sense of superiority and moral outrage. When did the woman caught in adultery feel the greatest gratitude towards Jesus? It was when her proposed stoning was cancelled.

And so, although it may sound a little self-indulgent, the plain truth is that I feel closest to God when I feel that I need him the most. And when I've wandered or marched into sinful stupidity, well, that would be the time when he's most needed.

Adrian, is there an anagram of your name? I have NASAL RAPIDS

I'm very slow sometimes. When I heard these words I thought it was a question followed by a rather plaintive request for sympathy. How dreadful to be suffering from something as disgusting as 'Nasal Rapids'. You'd never go out with a complaint like that. You'd have to buy shares in Kleenex, wouldn't you?

Yes, all right, I get it now. And I have to say that it's probably the best anagram of my awkward name that I've ever heard. So, well done whoever worked it out. My own efforts have been rather feeble. SPRAIN SALAD was one.

Such an eerily surreal combination of images. Even the great Salvador Dali might have hesitated to record it on canvas. Actually, when I look back to a family visit we once paid to the Dali museum in Figueras, I could be wrong about that. He would probably have enjoyed the challenge.

The only other one suggested to me was ASPIRIN SALAD, which is OK as far as it goes, but purists will immediately see the problem. The spelling has got to be spot on, hasn't it?

It's interesting how things like this catch on. I first started to do anagrams nearly thirty years ago when I was writing the weekly column that eventually became the original *Sacred Diary of Adrian Plass*. Gerald Coates was an anagram of GOD'S ALE CRATE. Eric Delve became VILE CREED. Disappointingly, Graham Kendrick could have been transmuted into GRANDMA KICKER if it hadn't been for that one superfluous 'h'. Incredibly annoying.

Readers began to send me their own anagrams, many of which were clever and fascinating. 'Forgiveness' could be rearranged to make SERVING FOES, 'mother-in-law' is, incredibly, an anagram of WOMAN HITLER, Elvis Presley becomes SILVERY SLEEP, and Armageddon, arrestingly, might also constitute AN ARMED GOD.

Most significantly of all, I would like to record for posterity the fact that 'love' is an anagram of VOLE, and the even more important fact that 'lost love' is an anagram of VOLE SLOT.

Need I say more? No, you're right.

When it comes to toilet paper, do you scrunch or fold?

This really is a most intensely personal question. No comment.

But I would like to commend a little toilet habit that I previously thought was disgusting. In many parts of Asia, toilet paper is not used at all, because people wash their nether regions with water. I used to think that was perfectly horrible, until a recent trip to Thailand taught me otherwise. Thai plumbing doesn't use the same diameter pipes as those found in the West, and toilet paper therefore causes the plumbing equivalent of a traffic jam. Thus they have nozzles next to the loo enabling one to pressure-wash one's undercarriage. This is actually far cleaner than our more primitive methods, and works well as long as the water is (a) pleasantly warm and (b) not shot out of the hose at 500 psi. If you do this and discover water seeping out of your ears, the pressure probably is set too high. And I am never going to talk about any of this again . . .

Do you have a favourite day of the week?

As I write, I have been alive for sixty-six years, five months and one day, which adds up to twenty-four thousand, two hundred and forty-one days altogether. Or to put it another way, I have enjoyed (or sometimes not enjoyed) three thousand, four hundred and sixty-three weeks. This means that I have experienced each day of the week on three thousand, four hundred and sixty-three occasions including today, which is a Monday.

Over all that time I have acquired some pretty strong views and impressions in connection with all seven days of the week. Here they are. Yours may be different, but that's quite OK. One man's Tuesday is another woman's Thursday, after all.

Monday is as grey and as flat as slate for most people. Even when it doesn't rain, it rains. Even when the sun shines, it rains. Even when there's a drought, it rains. Even when it's as dry as the driest thing in the history of the world – guess what? Yes, it rains.

Not on me, it doesn't. I work at home. I sit at my desk in my cosy study. Monday is as charmingly blue as a hedge-sparrow's egg. I like it, and it likes me. I stay dry. Even when it rains I enjoy watching it from my comfortable place. Have a good day at work, all you people who have to leave the house to go to work. Don't get too wet.

Tuesday is sort of plump and squishy. A day filled with jelly, that gets pushed into all sorts of shapes by people who suddenly realise that there are things left over from last Friday that should have been sorted out on Monday but weren't because they couldn't be bothered. Tuesday is green. Not a bright, happy green, but a shade less grim than the colour of mushy peas.

Wednesday is brown, like a creosoted fence. It is a rather grown-up day with a flat, stern, wooden, DIY sort of voice that tells you to get something practical done, for heaven's sake, before the whole week becomes a waste of time. Sometimes, unexpectedly, Wednesday evening dresses up and dances around a bit, but only if you've achieved a thing of some sort during the day. Between you and me, Wednesday is a bit up itself.

Thursday is a strange day. A unicorn of a day. Colour? Grey. Silvery grey. More exquisitely fine chain mail than heavy metal. Thursday is a woman, I think. She wafts and waves and beckons us on to the glittering path that will eventually take us to Friday.

Anything could happen on a Thursday. Sometimes it does.

Friday. Ah, Friday! Friday is a sizzling, fish-filled, crackling fire of a day, a good time to go to Bizzie Lizzie's in Skipton after work or school and have a Jumbo Haddock and Chips with Tuesday-coloured peas and bread and butter and a pot of tea. Aaaaah!

(I would love to know someone called Jumbo Haddock – an all-in wrestler perhaps? 'Hello, Jumbo,' I'd say, 'how's the wrestling? And how are you after all those half-nelsons and body-slams? And Mrs Haddock? How's she? And all the little sprats?')

Friday is the colour of embers in a hot fire. It wakes me up into realising that Wednesday can shout as loudly as it wishes from two days ago, but it won't make any difference, because Friday is whispering and buzzing in my ear, 'Don't you worry, the weekend is almost here . . .'

Friday evening is usually the best part of Saturday.

Saturday is yellow, almost golden, but not quite. The sandy beaches of Saturday are very alluring. A stroll in search of exotic shells. You almost never find them, but you might. Saturday plays a gentle tune of encouragement, but it also comes up with some jagged chords of challenge. Oh, Saturday, my friend, such tender, secret hopes I have placed in you over the years. Sometimes I have not been disappointed.

Why, oh why, do you hang around with that Sunday?

Sunday is a storm. Sometimes a dull storm, like unhappiness that never quite manages to cry, sometimes black skies with sudden, amazing flashes of white light. Sunday has an identity crisis, perhaps because of being squashed between Saturday and Monday.

'I think I could have been a Saturday,' says Sunday sadly. 'Actually, I think I was one once. I can't quite remember. Never mind. And just for the record, there's no way I'm responsible for Monday.'

Sunday is either God's day off, or mankind's day off. One or the other. Or both. No wonder it's confused.

So, there we are, then. Those are the days of my life. Good day to you.

My husband Graham is sure that when you two talk together in private your conversation is less circumspect than in public. Is it hard for you to sanitise your public utterings?

Well, if dear-but-suspicious Graham thinks that we enter-tain each other with horridly crude jokes, then he's quite wrong. But if he thinks that we are less reserved and more forthright in our private conversation than in public, then of course he's right.

While we're on the subject, sometimes Christian leaders rush to share unformed thoughts with the hapless public before they've had a chance to reflect fully or discuss them privately. And I have a huge 'pending' file of issues and doctrines where the theological jury inside my head is still considering its verdict.

But Graham's quite right. Plenty of the things Adrian and I talk about in private are never going to be shared in public. That's part of what authentic friendship is about.

Adrian, what inspired you to write another *Sacred Diary*?

The usual thing. Real life. From the middle of 2009 onwards, Bridget and I found ourselves closely involved in the resurrection of Scargill House, a Christian conference centre and intentional community in Yorkshire. It was a turbulent experience, filled with every extreme of emotion that you can possibly imagine. There were nights when we punched our pillows in anger and despair, and there were equally profound times of wide-eyed fascination or sheer relief as we began to see that our inadequacy was not going to be a barrier to the strange and unpredictable work of God among guests and community.

Once we had informality and a commitment to constructive uncertainty firmly in place, it seemed that anything was possible. The problem was, is, and will continue to be, maintaining that benevolent shapelessness in the face of a very human and understandable desire to construct one of those pleasantly harmless, rather point-less establishments where God's name appears prominently on the headed notepaper, but his role is quite definitely non-executive.

In my experience, hard times, hard work and holding your nerve always produce a lot of laughs. Patterns emerge. Things that seemed terribly important are revealed to be bewilderingly trivial. Small happenings

have unexpected and dramatically positive consequences. The tensions and contrasts, coupled with a sort
of perpetual puzzled fatigue, can produce laughter or
tears, or both.

After three years of observing these things, what could
I do? It was too tempting. I began to imagine a church
weekend set in a place similar to – but by no means the
same as – the one where we worked. From that moment
another *Sacred Diary* began its gestation, and I cannot tell
you what a delight it was to be reunited with some of my
old characters, as well as one or two new ones.

Will I ever write another one? No idea. Ask God. He
never tells me what to write when I ask, but he might tell
you. Let me know if you hear anything, won't you?

How would you describe God's sense of humour?

Vast. Ironic. Outrageous.

He made the inflatable cheeks of bullfrogs. And permanently irritated-looking rhinos. The horror-movie glare of
the moray eel. Me. Adrian.

Who is funnier, you or Jeff?

Cue endearing modesty.

We're both pretty odd in our own ways, but if your question is about being amusing I suppose we both have our moments. One of the major advantages of working together in public without a script is that each of us can pass a subject over to the other knowing that, at worst, he will say *something*, and at best, something very funny or very moving.

Perhaps this reflects the fact that, for better or worse, creatively we both operate out of a well of emotion. Spotting the funny side of things is probably the way in which we deal with being one layer of skin short of ever achieving consistent peace. And before I find myself batting away a buzzing swarm of ministry offers as a result of this statement, I am very happy with my dermatological deficiency, thank you very much. The benefits undoubtedly outweigh the disadvantages, especially for full-time writers who crave experiences as others crave physical nourishment.

Of course, Jeff may disagree with everything I've said in answer to this question, especially as, notwithstanding that endearing modesty of mine, he probably is more rampantly risible than me. On the other hand, he might go all bashful and deferential. He's funny like that.

Speaking of humour, it may be of interest to know that I have recently been writing groan-a-minute jokes. Why?

That is a mystery we shall all have to live in for now. Members of my family are suffering greatly, but the mania will soon pass, and in the meantime, have a look at a couple of sparkling examples.

A friend rang me in a panic because he'd locked himself inside a walk-in fridge. I said, 'I'll be there in a couple of hours. Just chill.'

I was never very good at understanding social nuances. I was at a dinner party a while ago. Twelve people. I asked the woman opposite me a question. She said, 'Snifty-don, snifty-moo, snifty-flea, snif-ty-snore, snifty-hive.' Tried again a bit later. She said, 'Blundered and gone, blundered and flue, blundered and tree, blundered and sore, blundered and drive.' I leaned across to the host and asked who she was. 'Oh, don't worry,' he said, 'she's just here to make up the numbers.'

Hilarious, eh? Now who's the funniest?

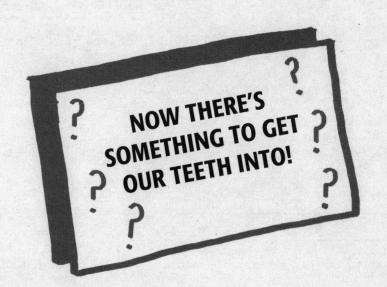

JEFF

Are there stories in the Bible that you really don't like? Do you have a least favourite Bible story?

I knew my answer on this one immediately – the Bible story in question is not so much disagreeable as downright horrifying. I hate it.

But then, I have a whole list of least favourite Bible stories. Sit tight – there's some nasty stuff coming.

It includes Abraham being told to take a knife and kill and burn his son Isaac. I can hardly stand to read it. I'm nauseated by Israel being commanded to create carnage as they took swords to the entire city of Jericho. Then there's the episode of Paul being less than gracious with errant John Mark and refusing to allow him to continue on his apostolic team. While there's not even a sniff of the violence that bleeds from the Abraham/Isaac and Jericho stories, this one makes me angry because Paul had received so much grace, what with him being the former chief persecutor of the Church and murderer of Christians (think ISIS with a fanatical Jewish face), and yet he seemed incapable of passing grace along and giving a young leader a second chance. It's a decision that disgusts me and, more importantly, disgusted his teammate Barnabas – their team split up that day and never reunited. Sad.

But my all-time least favourite episode is the vile story of Lot and his daughters. This awful incident includes incest and gang rape. Living in the moral cesspool that was Sodom, Lot is visited by some hunky angels. These celestial chaps are obviously rather handsome, because soon a group of men surround the house wanting to commit homosexual gang rape on them. If that isn't nasty enough – the picture of a mob of baying blokes crazed with violent lust is obscene – Lot's response to them is unspeakably worse.

He offers them his virgin daughters. I'll type that again, in case you missed the horror of it at first reading.

His bright idea was to throw his young, innocent daughters out to the wannabe rapists, and he even said that they could do whatever they liked with them.

What?

Commentators rush to talk about the cultural demands of hospitality – since they had come under his roof, Lot was honour-bound to protect the angels, at whatever price. Lot was under huge pressure, but there is absolutely no excuse for his shameless willingness to sacrifice his own family in this way. He was living in Sodom, but clearly, Sodom had taken up residence in him. Thankfully, his offer was not taken up.

But there's worse to come. This nasty, grubby, odious little man is mentioned in the New Testament, and when I read the description of him there, my mind revolts. Lot is described as 'righteous'.

Eh? A father who would surrender his own kith and kin to a hideous gang that would almost certainly not only have deflowered them, but killed them in the process?

But then that points to something remarkable about the gracious character of God.

Lot *was* righteous – in comparison to the amoral, oppressive, abusive people he lived alongside.

Samson was a bloodthirsty, headstrong womaniser, but he still ends up in the hallowed list of faith heroes in Hebrews 11.

Abraham twice pretended that his wife Sarah was not his wife, which led to all kinds of confusion and trouble. But in the New Testament, he is tagged repeatedly as the friend of God.

It seems that God does not define us by our worst moments or our most shameful thoughts, which is an enormous relief, considering the depths to which we can all sink without too much effort.

And so I really don't like the sickening story of Lot and his daughters at all. But when I look at God's verdict on that wimpish, cowardly, tormented man, I find strange relief from a terrible tale.

To return to one of the other stories that I mentioned – when God commanded Abraham to take a knife to Isaac – I've been pondering it over the last few days, and I am definitely warming to it. And that's because I'm thinking that it's actually an unfolding mini-drama about God showing Abraham what he *didn't* want.

Let me explain. I know that, at the heart of this gut-wrenching episode, there is a test of faith and obedience. God wanted to know if Abraham was serious about doing what he was told. Even though, as I said earlier, the New Testament constantly celebrates Abe as a man of faith and the friend of God (and barely mentions his failures), the Old Testament makes it clear that Abraham's walk of faith was a frankly unsteady amble with some major detours and lash-ups along the way. He struggled to live in the gap between God's promise and its fulfilment, and I sympathise with him. He had to wait twenty-five years between being told that he'd be the father of a nation and celebrating the birth of Isaac, who didn't show up until Abraham was a hundred years old.

Along the way, he stumbled, agreeing to sleep with a servant girl to produce a child. That was a decision that brought about sixteen years of domestic tension and then a painful parting as he had to disinherit Ishmael. And then he lied about his wife Sarah being his wife, twice, which meant that she was taken by other men, again with bad results all round.

So now he's told to kill the boy he loves, the son and heir he's waited decades for. He has to juggle this totally contradictory command with something else God has said: the nations will be blessed through Isaac. So what on earth is going on?

And then, when you dig around in the Bible, it's clear that God always hated human sacrifice. He judged his people when they fell into doing it, and sobs through the prophet Jeremiah, 'I did not command or mention [human sacrifice], nor did it enter my mind.'[1]

So what's the deal? God repeatedly railed against the horrific practice of people sacrificing children in worship. But now he commands Abraham to do just that. Why?

Abraham came from Ur, where people sacrificed children. He was heading for Canaan, where the same terrible rituals were used. So now God needed Abraham to know, once and for all, this is *not* what I want, ever.

---

1   Jeremiah 19:5

God could have just barked a command, a stern prohibition. But instead, he called Abraham to journey through the awful, conflicting agony of trekking up that mountain with his son and ultimately preparing him for death. Abraham now knew what excruciating emotional pain this hideous practice brought for both parent and child.

I think we need to talk a little more, not just about what God wants from us, but what he *doesn't* want. Some of my angst as a teenage Christian came from my desperate determination to do the will of God, which created an unhealthy obsessiveness, edging towards fanaticism. I was willing and ready to take the knife (figuratively speaking) to some very beautiful things in my life, just because I loved them so much. One of them was Kay, now my wife of thirty-six years. I agonised over loving her, because I loved her, and nearly lost her as I struggled.

Abraham was discovering that God calls us to trust him, not appease him. Back then, I was living in appeasement mode, thinking that God would love me more if I discarded what I loved the most, bringing my sacrifices to him. And I frequently still slip back into appeasement-thinking, wanting to buy God, to pay him off. But his love is not for sale. In a way that you and I can never fully understand (especially in the light of what we've just been thinking about), the price has been paid in full by Jesus.

Dennis Kinlaw preached a series of renewal services at a Wesleyan church here in Colorado, where I now live and work part of the time, back in 1982. He imagined God the Father and Jesus the Son watching the Abraham/Isaac drama end as God commanded Abraham to spare Isaac and offer a trapped lamb instead:

The Son said to the Father, 'We are going to be back here, aren't we?'

'Yes, Son, we are.'

'And this time there won't be a lamb in the thicket?'

'That's right, Son.'

'I am the Lamb.'

'You are the Lamb.'

And that's why Lot, that cowardly failure of a father, duplicitous Abraham with his sister-wife lies, the blustering, stern-faced Paul, and a host of other flawed and fragile souls like me and you – that's why we can count ourselves in when it comes to God and his grace.

Yes, I'm liking that Abraham story more and more . . .

Does it matter if I complain to God?

We wouldn't have inherited very many psalms if it did, would we? A large percentage of those ancient works of literature throb with emotions of anger, fear, betrayal and despair, and offer an informal invitation to all of us. Come on, tell it how it is. Tell God what you think of him. Sling some mud around, get it off your chest. Don't pull any punches.

The truth will be welcomed.

Do you believe that? Really? I think I do. There is a problem, though, for those of us who have drawn the outline of spiritual freedom but never got round to colouring it in. We so easily feel bullied and impeded by the neurotically positive culture that invades churches and usurps true faith when it begins to look as though some cherished pet version of Christianity just isn't working out.

> Brothers, sisters, sing and shout,
> Drown the troubled questions out.

People sometimes use the phrase 'dishonouring God' to describe the negative responses, fear, anger and despair that sweep over us when none of the promises seem to be kept, and we simply don't feel like the cherished children of a loving father.

Personally, I have no intention of being buried under all this rubbishy denial stuff any more. I do want to honour God, and I believe one way of doing that is to make sure that I take my tears, complaints, disappointments or feelings of betrayal straight to him. He may have plenty of things to say back to me, but that's fine. I would rather have an honest row with God than anger him by placing useless fire on his altar, the kind of fake and feeble sacrifice that you can read about in the first chapter of Malachi if you wish.

The writer of Psalm 88, a man who has clearly reached the end of his rope, ends his lyrical catalogue of pain by declaring bluntly, 'darkness is my closest friend'. No positive little upturn in this one, is there?

What do the unhappy psalmists have in common? It may be almost too obvious to see.

'Where would a man hide a leaf?' asks Father Brown.

'In a forest,' replies his friend Flambeau.

'And where would he hide a pebble?'

'On a beach.'

And where, I ask, would you hide a man who speaks honestly to God?

You would hide him in the psalms, I reply to myself.

This is the thing that all these sufferers have in common: whatever the darkness that envelops them, whatever is boiling inside them, whatever the collision between expectation and experience, they lay it out before the one true God, and wait to see what he will or will not do.

Of course, the idea is not that we should behave like young people away from home for the first time, phoning home to unload all their woes onto a long-suffering parent and forgetting to mention the good bits. Love, gratitude, sorrow, hope – all of these things also feature in the psalms, and it would be good to express them as well, but only if we can do it honestly.

In our work with groups and individuals, Bridget and I sometimes encourage people to write psalms for themselves. Paradoxically, the release of negative emotions can have a very positive effect. The lines that follow are my feeble attempt to offer a model of honesty that they can follow.

I didn't hear you knocking
I didn't hear you knocking
How loudly did you knock?
See, I might have been upstairs
Or in the garden

Walk down the path beside the house next time
And call across the fence
What about the bell?
There is a bell
You didn't use the bell
Behold I stand at the door and ring the bell
Are bells not scriptural or something?
Bells are made for man
Not man for bells
Don't you think?
Sometimes I am shocked from sleep
By sounds that I could swear
Are made by urgent knuckles on a door
So scary in the middle of the night
I never had the nerve to creep downstairs
And hover trembling in the chilly hall
Trying to be brave enough to face the night
The thought of what I might let in was terrifying
Was that sometimes you?
Did I miss you then?
Or was it always just a dream?
And if it is a metaphor
This knocking thing
The problem is
I cannot tell where my imagination ends
And your voice calling to my heart begins
Too many thoughts and questions close me down
A thousand voices whisper
'He will never come'
And all too often
Far too often
Disappointment wins

What do you fear most?

I know it's both a famous quote and a cliché, but what I most fear is fear.[2] I know people who are navigating through the most harrowing circumstances, but do so generally with a sense of peace and even authentic joy. So I don't think it's what happens in life that we have to fear, but rather our reaction to what happens that is critical.

A few weeks ago, I learned once again that fear has an incredible capacity for exaggeration, and that it mugs us most effectively in the small hours of the night.

I was preaching in Malaysia, at a stunning church packed full of enthusiastic souls whom I found a little intimidating. For one thing, a high proportion of them wore skinny jeans and were epically cool. More importantly, they are following Jesus in a Muslim-majority culture where it's illegal to reach out to any follower of Islam, which 99 per cent of Malays are. It's reported that there are 'correction camps' where Malay Christian converts are taken to forcibly rehabilitate them, and occasionally government spies show up at the church gatherings. The church I visited embarrassed me with their commitment and passion.

---

2 'The only thing we have to fear is fear itself.' (Franklin D. Roosevelt, First Inaugural Address, 1933)

We briefly went to Thailand, and then had to fly back to Malaysia and stay overnight there before connecting to our return flight to the UK. Checking in at an airport hotel, I was initially pleased, but then a little taken aback by the warm smile from the chap at reception.

A surprising conversation unfolded.

HIM: Name please, sir?

ME: Lucas – Jeff and Kay.

HIM: Oh, welcome to you both. Mr Lucas, you're a big man.

ME: (*Suddenly (a) self-conscious about the fact that I have piled on rather too many pounds due to my over-indulgence in the Malaysian national pastime of eating, but (b) equally weighing the possibility that his comment referred to the fact that people from the West are gener-ally taller than our Asian friends*) What?

HIM: No, I mean . . . you're famous. I looked up your website earlier. You're a well-known Christian leader. You've written lots of books. I know who you are, sir.

ME: Right. OK. Thank you.

Looking back on the episode, I'm convinced that he was simply being nice, although it seems a little strange to do a background check on a guest at a hotel.

When I awoke with a start at 2 a.m., that's not how I saw it. Here's a sample of my rambling, idiotic thoughts.

That check-in experience was really weird. Perhaps he wasn't just being kind. Perhaps, in this culture where Islam is firmly in control, he was thinking that he might benefit from contacting a radical group and then, for a payoff, he could invite them to come and get us . . .

At this point I reached for my phone, googled 'ISIS, Malaysia', and discovered that there are indeed ISIS cells operating there, and that they had just issued threats against Kuala Lumpur.

That's it. He's going to call his friends at ISIS. There's going to be a knock on the door at any moment, and we'll be led away, screaming – but ignored by the other hotel guests because they're too terrified to intervene. I'm going to die . . .

So I got out of bed, checked the locks on the door, and noticed with dismay that we were on the eighth floor, which meant we couldn't leap out of the window when the masked men came for us . . .

OK. The reality is that we were never under threat, and I'm embarrassed to report all of this. But it does show the power of fear, which seeks to imprison us with threats of awful possibilities, most of which will never happen.

There was a useful side-effect from my ridiculous panic in the middle of the night. I realised that there are people who live, every day and every night, with the genuine possibility that they might have hostile visitors at their door any minute, and all just because they love and follow Jesus. How brave they are, and how they need our prayers, and our voices to speak out on their behalf. Their fear, unlike mine, is based on reality.

Jeff, does anything annoy you about Adrian?

I'm glad that this question landed with me, because it means Adrian doesn't get a chance to vent about what is probably a somewhat lengthy list of things about me that irritate him. There are just three things that annoy me about St Adrian, and the irritations have been long-lived, niggling away at me ever since I met him, back in 1869 or thereabouts.

Firstly, and most frustratingly, Adrian can see through me in a millisecond. Driving together while on tour, I started to describe how a fellow Christian leader had deeply hurt me. Having poured out my somewhat embittered heart, I affirmed that I was no longer bothered or concerned about the whole incident.

There was a momentary silence, and then Adrian snorted a little snort, and finally started to laugh out loud. What insensitivity to my pain! And then, ever so gently (because Adrian is relentlessly gentle), he murmured, 'Of course, Jeff. It doesn't hurt you even the tiniest little bit now, does it?' My cover was blown. So, it can be annoying not to be able to pull the wool over his eyes. But it's rather wonderful too.

My second gripe with Mr Plass is this: he writes far better than I ever can. Some of his emails (that is, when he gets around to sending them – there's another source of annoyance) are sheer poetry. That kind of turn of phrase flows from the heart and mind of a true wordsmith.

Oh, and a third, though more trivial, niggle. Very occasionally, he spills food down himself when eating, although it may be that he's saving a snack for later, so perhaps this is intentional.

Do you talk about Jesus when you're not on a platform?

Not as much as I'd like. In this area of my life, I aspire to become more like my friend Larry.

Larry is a hairdresser. My hairdresser.

Hairdressers make great evangelists.

For one thing, they have a captive audience, and are keen to go beyond the standard conversational fodder that they (and taxi drivers everywhere) have to endure. 'So, have you been busy?' And then, hairdressers are trusted with the precious commodity that is hair, so clients are more likely to trust them to discuss matters of the soul.

Most importantly, hairdressers make good evangelists for one simple reason.

They're armed.

OK, scissors have limited potential as a weapon, but in the right hands, they can be lethal, hence encouraging a more attentive response to a Jesus-loving stylist on a mission from God.

Larry, who painstakingly tries to shape my decreasingly hirsute peninsula into something stylish, is gifted at sharing the good news of the faith with his clients.

But recently the tables were turned for me. I became somewhat evangelistic, and the chap cutting my hair was the eager listener. Now, this was something of an answer to prayer, because my attempts at sharing my faith over the last decade or so have been somewhat lacking. In missional terms, I had lost my voice. Reacting to the over-zealous, cringeworthy evangelistic techniques of my earliest years as a Christian, when I would delightedly buttonhole strangers and inflict a breathless monologue upon them (regardless of whether they were interested, intrigued or even awake), I had fallen quiet on the evangelistic front. Many of us have done precisely the same. Excusing ourselves by the oft-used quotation, 'Preach the gospel at all times; when necessary, use words', some of us have packed up on using words altogether. But the chap who said that first was none other than St Francis of Assisi, famous not only for chatting with squirrels, but also for giving away everything that he owned. When you've donated all you have to the poor because of your love for Jesus, you probably don't have to use words so much.

So I've been asking God to help me speak out a little more. And last week, away from home, I walked into an unfamiliar hairdressers at random, and was taken aback by the immediate opportunity I had to share my faith. So quickly did the hairdresser start asking me questions about Christianity, I forgot to say how I wanted him to cut my hair. Enjoying chatting about the difference between dead religion and living faith, I was distracted, and then I removed my glasses, so I couldn't see what was happening in the mirror. Spec-less, I'm as blind as the proverbial bat (actually blinder, seeing as I'm not equipped with sonar). He got to work with the clippers. Somewhat enthusiastically.

Twenty minutes later, I put my glasses back on nervously, to be greeted by the reflection of a chap who looked like a new recruit to the US Marines. I realised just how short it was when I walked back to the church where I was speaking later that evening and a lady volunteer (whom I'd met earlier in the day with a fuller complement of hair) greeted me by saying, 'Gosh. Who did that to you?' My wife welcomed me with a look of sheer horror that proves that her eyes are in full working order, followed by a sympathetic smile that proves that her compassionate heart still works too.

But here's what happened. I'd invited the hairdresser to come to church that night, and gave him some books, quite expecting that he wouldn't show. Oh me of little faith. But he did come. He came up to me afterwards and told me that he'd enjoyed the evening, had signed up for Alpha, and had agreed to meet the minister for coffee later that week. I would later joke that I laid down my hair for the sake of the gospel (although there was never that much to lay down). But I recovered something far better: the authentic joy of having a natural, non-pushy conversation that will hopefully help someone discover how much God loves them.

And so, I'm getting my voice back, ever so slowly. And hopefully, one bright, beautiful day, I'll grow my hair back too.

Our curate always says 'God told me' very confidently. What wavelength is he tuned into? This never happens to me.

A thought: have you checked that 'God' isn't your curate's nickname for the vicar? Just wanted to flag that up as a possibility. Curates can become quite ironical in tone as they acquire confidence and are healed of porphyrophobia (look it up for yourself).

But seriously – it is a bit of a problem, isn't it? I have written elsewhere about a man in a church we once attended who sometimes used part of the service to relay the conversations he had enjoyed with God over the marmalade that morning. I put it like that because that's how it sounded.

'God said to me, "Alan, have you thought about the fact that you and your family are usually late for church?" And I said to him, "No, not really." And he said to me, "Well, I think you should." And I said to God, "OK, I will." And he said, "Good, thank you, Alan." And then I said . . .'

These gripping episodes of Alan's spiritual soap opera lasted for quite a long time on occasions, and they had a rather stultifying effect on the rest of the congregation. We sat and listened with a sort of dull resignation; some, no doubt, because they felt like you listening to your curate.

Why, they asked themselves, am I excluded from this amazing world where Almighty God speaks in chattily conversational tones over the breakfast table? All our problems must surely be over if dialogue like this really is available. Between John Humphrys and God, it should be possible to get conclusive answers to just about any question under the sun before nine o'clock in the morning at the latest.

Others among us, myself included, sat wriggling our toes and grinding our teeth in silent anguish, trapped between the demands of politeness and appropriate restraint, and a burgeoning desire to stand up and tell Alan he was talking a load of cobblers. Are you seriously telling us, we were bursting to ask, that the eternal mystery of man's relationship with God has now been solved because the Creator drops in on a daily basis for a one-to-one planning meeting with Alan Moresby at 38 Charlton Gardens? Or what? Eh?

The problem, you see, was that we were all, theoretically at least, signed up to the notion that God does indeed speak to ordinary people in ordinary situations. Someone was always on about it. 'When you're praying,' a minister or elder would say with coy severity, 'don't just talk. Listen as well. Let God get a word in edgeways.'

Christian tittering usually followed this piece of daring high humour.

Through a chorus conclusively proving that the devil does not have all the best songs, the children of the church were taught that 'prayer is like a telephone'. Well, it's not, is it? With a telephone you dial the correct number, wait for a bit, and then the person you've called speaks to you. You have a conversation. You don't have to concentrate hard to see if you can detect a message in the silence. For Moses and Jesus prayer might have been like a telephone, but for most of us, it's not.

Being able to hear God's voice is one of a longish list of faux certainties, unofficial articles of faith that are spoken with confidence but privately infused with unease, encouraging us to dilute the truth. The adoption and reinforcement of these dangerous unrealities will inevitably produce Christian institutions lacking in real power.

It's unlikely that I have actually met the curate mentioned in this question, and I have no idea if God speaks clearly to him or not, but my warning to myself and everyone else is that, as ever, the truth will set us free. In the context of hearing from God, these are the ways in which I have tried my best to stay within the truth.

First of all, I can see no reason, generally speaking, why any kind of authenticity tag has to be attached to the things we might say to people. We all know the familiar phrases:

'I feel the Lord is saying . . .'

'God has laid something on my heart to share with you . . .'

'The Holy Spirit is giving me a Scripture verse that will speak into your situation . . .'

These garishly bejewelled attachments to unadorned advice may help the would-be prophet feel a little more confident in speaking out, but in making these claims we are telling people that they are responsible directly to God for the way in which they respond. I don't know about you, but I find that a very sobering thought. Experience suggests that, in the main, if you have something to say that might be from God, it makes little difference whether you put a label on it or not. Why not leave off the label? If it's from God it will do its work; if it's not it might still be useful, but it certainly won't add an extra burden to the person you're trying to help.

Yes, of course there may be times when a more modern version of the old 'Thus saith the Lord' stuff does the trick, but we do need to be careful.

When I want to tell people about something that I believe (and hope) God has said to me, I normally preface it with the words, 'If God really does speak to people, and if he really did speak to me on this occasion, this is what he said . . .' Even if I am fairly sure, and every now and then I almost am(ish), none of the force is lost by leaving a small window open for doubt. People need to be able to breathe.

My final piece of advice to the person who asked this question is as follows. If you want to hear the voice of God, don't role-play being a Christian, don't make anything up, keep asking him to speak to you, and look forward to the intriguing complications that a positive answer to this prayer will introduce into your life.

What story/anecdote have you told and then regretted afterwards?

I used to tell what I (wrongly) thought was a rather witty story about an over-enthusiastic Christian I met at Bible college. It wasn't funny, it was cruel, and I've often wondered if my careless remarks ever got back to that person. In case you're wondering, I'm not going to tell the story here and compound my stupidity. Engaging brain (and heart) before opening mouth is a vital lesson of life.

Do you dance?

Yes. Horribly. I've got rhythm, but not much coordination, so I look like someone who is suffering some kind of fit. It's not a pretty sight.

But if it's OK, I'd love to tell you about two of the most beautiful sights I've ever seen in my life, both of which took place on the dance floor.

The first was at the wedding of our daughter Kelly to Ben. It was an emotionally charged day, with me blubbing through my brief father-of-the-bride speech, and then Kelly devastating me (in the most beautiful way) with her own speech. I'll never forget these three sentences: 'Some of you here know my dad as a Christian leader, and you might be wondering what he is like in private. Well, I'm here to tell you that he's the same guy. I love you, Dad.'

But then, after a meal of chicken curry and Ben and Jerry's ice cream (not together), the DJ spun his magic and the dancing began. And it was then that Kelly took the hands of her two grandmothers – both reserved women, who wouldn't dream of stepping onto a dance floor – and leapt around with them as Sister Sledge hollered, 'We are family.' We were, and we are.

The second beautiful dance happened just a few weeks ago. My mother, one of the grandmothers I have just mentioned, no longer remembers that we are family. Bewildered by the fog that is dementia, she is now in residential care. Sometimes, when I visit her, she remembers who I am. Sometimes she does not, and occasionally she thinks that I'm her eighty-year-old friend Audrey. And then we've had those difficult chats when, not realising who I am, she complained *to* me *about* me. I suppose it's one way to find out what people really think about you . . .

I've learned so much about incarnation from being around my mum, because now I have to comprehensively enter her world, ignore mine and put the real world on hold for a while. I lie to her all the time. When she asks me how my dad is doing, I tell her that he is just fine. For a while, I tried telling her that he died over twenty years ago, but that just agitates her – and worse, she suffers grief all over again, because she has forgotten that he is dead. Struggling with palming her untruths, I was greatly helped by Louis Theroux's documentary on dementia. Interviewing the senior manager of a special care centre for dementia sufferers, he asked if the staff told lies to the patients in order to spare them distress. 'Of course we do,' she smiled. 'Here, we lie all day long!'

Anyway, Kay and I went to see Mum just before Christmas. A jolly lady dressed as Santa was crooning Christmassy classics to backing tracks, and suddenly she invited the residents – some of whom were barely aware that she was singing, and others of whom were asleep – to dance if they'd like. Some of the care staff invited residents to dance, and so there were now three or four couples meandering very slowly around the room.

'Why don't you dance with your mum?' said Kay. I didn't much like the idea. Helpfully, neither did Mum.

'No, thank you,' she retorted, rather huffily. I love my mum, but she has had a lifelong ability to be huffy, one that has survived her dementia. She then immediately fell asleep.

About five minutes later, she suddenly woke up, bright as a button, and for no reason that I can think of, grabbed my hand and said, 'Come on, let's dance.'

And so we did. It was surely not a pretty sight, as we shuffled around the room to Mariah Carey singing 'Have yourself a merry little Christmas'.

I need to pause for a moment.

Something has happened to me, just now, as I sit here tapping away at the computer keyboard. As I recalled that dance with my mum, an experience surfaced in my mind that I believe is my earliest memory.

I don't recall much about my childhood. Sometimes I think the brain has a sealed vault, where files full of conversations and tears and anxieties and Christmases are stored in the organic equivalent of old grey metal filing cabinets.

Perhaps I don't remember much because, frankly, it wasn't so great. Our home was not terribly happy or peaceful – and little wonder. My mother had a scowling stepfather, a road worker with a cruel tongue. He wore a thick leather belt which held up his trousers and, by all accounts, helped him control his stepdaughter, my mum. The bruises on her soul have been lifelong.

And then she met my dad. After being captured in North Africa at the beginning of the Second World War, he spent four years of his young life rotting in a prisoner of war camp, just a few miles from Auschwitz. Taken on a death march in the coldest winter in a hundred years, he finally escaped.

Back in England, my mum and dad actually first met at a dance. After asking my mum to go out with him, my dad walked into the pub where the navvy with the thick belt used to down ten pints most nights.

Their first meeting didn't go well.

My step-grandfather told my dad that he didn't like soldiers, because they all carried sexually transmitted diseases.

My dad informed my step-grandfather that if he ever used a belt on his daughter again, he would kill him.

An ex-POW, and a young woman who had learned to be scared of men. The fact that these two parents of mine found each other and managed to stay together is remarkable. There were some good times in our home, but a lot of tension and conflict too.

But I *do* remember another dance. I was very small, perhaps two years old, and Dad was playing one of his favourite songs on the gramophone. Suddenly he picked me up, settled my head on his shoulder, and began to dance around the room with me, very slowly, very gently. I can smell the Brylcreem that he used on his hair. I can feel his hand on the back of my head, gently nestling my head into the side of his neck. I can hear him humming the song into my ear. It felt good. Safe.

Nearly six decades later, just for a while, dancing with her son, everything was safe for my mum, everything was as it should be. For a moment at least, she really was having herself a merry little Christmas. No conflict. No belt.

I keep the photo of the two of us on my phone. The way things are going, it may well be that our Christmas dance turns out to be our very last dance. And I'll never be able to listen to Mariah Carey sing that song without shedding a tear.

But I'm glad we shared that awkward little waltz together.